I Am Living Heaven On Earth

Melissa Drum

Copyright © 2020 Melissa Drum. All rights reserved. No part of this book can be reproduced in any form without written permission of the author and its publisher.

"I Am that I Am!" (Exodus 3:14)
+ "Thy will be done on Earth, as it is in Heaven" (Matthew 6:10).
= #iamlivingheavenonearth

Contents

Introduction 4
Part One: Life Before 7
   1: A Seeker Within 8
   2: Needing Help 10
   3: The Gift of Reading 12
   4: Turning Point 13
Part Two: Guided 14
   5: Ask, Believe, Receive 15
   6: Gratitude 16
   7: The Most Important Thing 18
   8: To Believe in Miracles 19
   9: Live Out the Example 20
   10: Vision Boards 21
   11: Balance 23
   12: Intuition 25
   13: Sweet Boy 27
   14: Lifelong Messenger 29
   15: The Choice to Stand in Faith 31
Part Three: The Journey 32
   16: Our Bodies, Our Temples 33
   17: The Magic of Asheville 34
   18: The Meaning of Melissa 37
   19: Positive Thoughts & Expectations 39

20: Moai Angel Sisters 40
Part Four: Turning Within 42
21: Union 43
22: Muladhara..44
23: Svadhisthana..46
24: Manipura..47
25: Anahata..48
26: Vishuddhi...49
27: Ajna 50
28: Sahasrara..51
29: A Vessel of Love & Peace...........................53
30: Nourishing Our Bodies 55
31: Primary Foods...58
Part Five: Living Deeply 59
32: Moving Mountains 60
33: The Gap 62
34: Our Inner Holiness......................................64
35: A Vision of the Night 66
Part Six: Nosara..67
36: In Harmony...68
37: A Trip to Remember...................................70
38: To First Heal Ourselves..............................72
39: Divine Appointment 75
Part Seven: I AM 76
40: God Within Us..77

41: The Resurrection & The LIfe 79
42: The Third Word 81
43: The Secret to Creating Miracles 83
44: To Live in the Feeling................................. 85
45: Loving Ourselves.. 86
46: The Kingdom of God Within You............. 87
47: The Meek & Egoless 89

Part Eight: Living Heaven on Earth 91
48: Meant to Shine.. 92
49: Bridging Heaven & Earth 94
50: Our Personal Legend 96
51: Religion of Love 97
52: An Instrument of Thy Peace 98
53: The Violet Flame 100
54: With My Deepest Gratitude...................... 103

Author's Favorites 105

Author's Thank yous 110

Introduction

🕊🕊🕊

I often wonder how Exodus 3:14 and Matthew 6:10 have become so misunderstood. Everyone talks about how much better Heaven is going to be, and how their pains and sorrows will be no more once they die. Yet, we live in Heaven or Hell every day on Earth by our thoughts and by our daily choices. Heaven and Hell are states of consciousness. We are meant to live in Heaven on Earth! Jesus and other great teachers demonstrated this by setting the example and left their wisdom in written books.

When you wait to have joy later by saying things such as, "In Heaven, things will be better," you separate yourself from living Heaven on Earth, now! You live for a fantasy of what might be, or of what might come. By doing this you waste the precious gift of life that is happening here and now.

I love how Eckhart Tolle puts it when he says: "The mind is a superb instrument if used rightly. Used wrongly, however, it becomes very destructive. To put it more accurately, it is not so much that you use it wrongly—you usually don't use it at all. It uses you. This is the disease. You believe that you are your mind. This is the delusion. The present moment holds the key to liberation. But you cannot find the present moment as long as you are your mind. Ego=Edging God Out!"

According to *A Course in Miracles*, a self-study program that guides the reader into spiritual transformation, the job of the Ego is to seek, but never to find. It distracts us from the truth that the happiness that we are all looking for has always been within us. The Ego has an insatiable need for more and more, without ever acknowledging the present moment as the greatest gift. Enlightenment, however, is when all of one's knowledge comes to the forefront of their Being. The main focus of attention to the enlightened person is the now, or the present. Once again, Eckhart Tolle states it best: "We fall out of alignment with our universal purpose if our focal point is not in the present moment. Realizing that the present moment is all that you really ever have. Now is the most precious thing there is."

As I sit down to write, one red cardinal sits perched at my window sill, chirping at me, obviously trying to get my attention. The word *cardinal* comes from the Latin word cardo, meaning hinge or axis. Like a door's hinge, cardinals are known for opening the gap between Earth and Spirit, and for bringing the wisdom of the Universe to one's doorstep. They have long been held as the most notable of spiritual messengers.

This brings a heaviness to my eyes as I embark on this journey. Sitting for long periods of time is definitely out of my comfort zone, and reading and writing were my worst subjects in school, but there is a fire burning inside me that I cannot ignore; the call and vision are speaking so loud and clear.

Tears roll down my cheeks as I gather myself to share my heart to the world.

It is the vulnerable heart that breaks broken hearts free.

—ANN VOSKAMP

Part One: Life Before

A Seeker Within

I remember a few years ago when my life was spiraling out of control and I, too, was lost. I was not living—I was surviving. I would lay my head down at night, and I would whisper to my husband, "Do you think our hard work will ever pay off?"

He would whisper back, "I sure hope it's not all for naught."

Before dozing off to sleep I would think to myself, *Surely, my present life cannot be what the next seventy-plus years will be like. There has to be more to life than what I have experienced and witnessed so far.* I decided that I had to become a seeker, as I believed that there had to be secrets to life that I have not yet discovered. It was fitting, because as Matthew 7:7 says, "Seek and you will find."

During this time, my husband Jason and I both were struggling with severe anxiety. We both own a floor-covering company, in addition to being parents of two wonderful children. While we were proud of the lives we had created, it didn't take away the fact that we were overwhelmingly busy. It didn't help that throughout my life, I had been labeled OCD and ADD. It didn't matter that I was a wanderlust. It didn't matter that I was a seeker. It didn't matter that I was an alchemist. Over time, I had started simply to believe what I had been labeled, over the divine truths of who I am within. For the longest time, I went through life thinking that there was something wrong with everyone in the world, including myself. But, I can honestly say today that this is the farthest from the truth. Life is magical! It was my thoughts and energy that I was giving that was creating my reality.

During this busy time, however, Jason and I would arise every morning at 4:30 am. We would spend this time at the gym, as this was the only time we had alone together. It was refreshing to go someplace where no one would need us, nor disturb us. Outside of the gym, though, I would spend my life in a daze. I felt myself going through the motions as the days went on, hardly experiencing true happiness and fulfillment.

Similarly, I didn't experience much happiness either in my childhood. I was raised in a religious Pentecostal household, with parents that would take us to church twice on Sundays and once every Wednesday night. After twenty years of marriage, however, my religious parents divorced. The day my mom left the marriage, I told her she taught me two valuable lessons in life: to never rely on anyone, but myself; and to never turn my back on God.

These things from my childhood, though, left me unsure of my feelings about religion as I became an adult. My husband could understand my sentiments. He had lost his father a year before we met, which didn't really affirm his faith in any way. All and all, we just did not get it. We would visit different churches every so often, but never felt the pull to go every Sunday, nor to be fully involved.

Surprisingly, there were a few Bible verses from my childhood that stuck with me throughout the years. One being: "Seek ye first the kingdom of God and His righteousness and all these things shall be added unto you" (Matthew 6:33). And another: "In all your ways, acknowledge Him, and He will direct your path" (Proverbs 3:6). I've often pondered on these verses and wondered: *What if these really are true?*

I figured that at this point, I didn't have much to lose. I was mentally, physically, and emotionally tired of trying to figure things out on my own. The daily grind of a busy life was draining and exhausting me.

🕊🕊🕊
Needing Help

Soon after, I had decided that I was going to pray every morning at the gym, while I was on the treadmill. I didn't even know how to pray, or for what exactly I was praying. I just knew I needed help! My initial prayers were for guidance and direction, and like anything else, the more I practiced it, the better I became; and eventually, my actions became a daily habit. I prayed every day for about six months before I started to see that some magic was beginning to happen.

I was in my kitchen one morning, and my husband came to me and wrapped me in his arms. It felt deeper than it had in quite some time. It felt magical, actually!

"What made you do that?" I asked.

He told me that he wasn't really sure. I looked at him with tears in my eyes, and told him, "I have been praying for our relationship,"

Our relationship wasn't necessarily in trouble, but I was aware that the business of the life that we had created together definitely had caused our marriage to be put on the bottom of the priority list. As we went about our day, we said nothing else about our magical experience from that morning.

At this point, we had no extra time for our families, nor our friends. Throughout my life, I never felt like I could fit in, or that anyone could truly understand me, anyway. However, giving our lives to our children and to our business created quite a bit of loneliness, one that seemed to span over several years.

When it came to our children, my husband and I both found it incredibly important that they participated in whatever sport their hearts desired. This desire came from the absence of sports from our childhoods due to financial reasons. I remember daydreaming as a child, that I was an amazing dancer like my friends. I also remember being disheartened watching my friends advance confidently in their God-given abilities, while I was on the sidelines being their cheerleader.

My dad always told me that it was too expensive to participate in my desired sport. He, instead, allowed me to be on the track and cross country team with my sister, as it was an inexpensive sport with little time commitment. I was a fast runner, but running was not my passion. I ran for seven years and decided to quit during my junior year of high school. My father and running coach both felt disappointed at my decision. My skills were good enough to earn me a running scholarship that would have paid for my college. Still, I decided that the time had come for me to listen to my own intuition. I was running for the enjoyment of others, but not for myself. And I desired something more. Much, much more!

At the time my life spiraled out of control, my children were doing multiple sports apiece. My son played football in the fall, basketball in the winter, and played on a year-round traveling baseball team. He also would play golf—his passion—during any free time he had. There were times where his sports overlapped one another, and this was when I was really crazy. My daughter was on a dance competition team and also played golf in her free time.

    I was the one getting both of them from point A to point B. I was also the one preparing breakfast, lunch, and dinner in our home; doing all the laundry; and helping with the business as much as I could, on top of all the other household chores. My children had little time to assist with any household duties due to their school and sports schedules. I would spend an average of four hours a day in the car, and an average of four hours a day in the kitchen. My husband was working an average of ten to twelve hours a day keeping our business afloat. Needless to say, we had very little time, and had accumulated a lot of financial responsibilities at that point.

The Gift of Reading

Somehow in the business of this all, my husband and I were able to squeeze in a date night with one of our couple friends for whom we rarely had time. Our friend was a person who held his doctorate in business, and someone we often consulted for advice. During the evening, he told us about a Steve Jobs biography that he was listening to on the Audible app, and about how he was thoroughly enjoying Audible itself. He told us of how this had made his commutes back and forth to work much more enjoyable than they had been.

This had really intrigued me, because one of my biggest fears as a mother was losing myself and relying completely on a man. In addition, I was fond of the idea of being productive while I was spending an exorbitant amount of time on the road in the car. With these thoughts in mind, I downloaded the app the following day.

I started with the Steve Jobs book that my friend had loved and highly praised. I thought, *What better biography than this one?* The book was a good read, but it didn't speak to my soul. Still, I desired to help my husband grow our business, so I continued listening to books within that category. My original plan was to listen to a business book, then a self-help book, and then a parenting book. However, there came a point when I was bored with business books as they were not fulfilling me, which led me back to the verse: "In all your ways acknowledge Him, and He will direct your path" (Proverbs 3:6). Soon, I began praying that I would be lead to the right books.

In the meantime, I figured out that the self-help books were speaking to me on a more-enriching level than any others I have read. They drew me in so much, that I became consumed, finding myself listening to them while driving, working out, doing laundry, and even while cooking dinner. Every adult interaction from then on revolved around

Audible and book recommendations. As exciting as it was, this new interest in books was actually foreign to me. I had disliked reading as a child, and books had typically bored me. I remember feeling annoyed as I would read the same lines over and over again, but still not retaining the information. Additionally, I had told myself that I could never be a focused reader because of the ADD labels I had come to believe about myself.

I never understood how people liked to read until now! I realized that we all have different interests and this was a game-changer. I would tell my husband, "Even as a small child, you know what your interests are." This is why I never liked reading as a child: the books I had read were the wrong ones for me. I started buying my children books that I knew would interest them and guess what? They would read them!

Turning Point

And then, magic happened: I was led to a friend: Silvia Saey. Our paths intertwined on several occasions within the last few years, and we followed each other on social media, but that was the extent of our relationship. She is the owner of her own company named Good Tidings. From being with her, one can tell that she has a deep love for authentic beauty, especially the ones possessed by Southwestern and Native American cultures. Her company specializes in designing Navajo-inspired bags, blankets, and jewelry crafted from a special kind of mineral: Turquoise.

Turquoise, the oldest stone in man's history, is the talisman of kings and warriors. It is a stone of wholeness and integration, assisting us to pull all of our experiences together and glean wisdom. It combines sweetness and sophistication while prompting inner strength; it is the mark of the spiritual warrior. It is also the ultimate way of showing respect to ancestors who have passed on. Turquoise also symbolizes protection and good luck.

I admired how my new friend knew the power of this incredible mineral, and had incorporated it into her life and business. I knew I felt something wonderfully different about this woman. Good tidings are even mentioned in the Bible: "I bring you good tidings of great joy which will be to all people" (Luke 2:10). Now, I know this is how God is using her company.

The business my husband and I owned was doing some floors for her home because she was preparing to sell. My husband had me drop some carpet samples off with her, which is something that I didn't typically do. After Silvia invited me in, we came into her library. From the shelf, she pulled out two books that had grabbed my attention, and asked me if I had read them. I told her that I hadn't, although I knew immediately that I had been led to these books.

After leaving her home, I bought *The Power* on Audible, and ordered *The*

Magic because it only comes in paperback. The author is Rhonda Byrne, the television writer, and producer who created the documentary *The Secret*. She also wrote the book of the same name, as well as its successors—*The Power, The Magic*, and *Hero*. For over a decade, she has been regarded as one of the most spiritually influential people of our time.

 I started listening to *The Power* immediately, and I was captivated. I could feel the magic in Rhonda's voice! It consumed me, and I knew that this was the turning point in my life.

*Part Two:
Guided*

Ask, Believe, Receive

I finished *The Power, The Secret*, and *Hero* within one month. *The Power* is about the power of love. *The Secret* is about the three-step process: ask, believe, and receive, which is based on a quotation from the Bible: "And all things, whatsoever ye shall ask in prayer, believe, and ye shall receive" (Matthew 21:22). *Hero* reveals that each of us is born with everything we need to live our greatest life and that by doing so, we will fulfill our mission and purpose.

Reading these had opened up life for me in the most amazing of ways. My husband could feel the energy in my voice and noticed the change in my aura. I was living in a state of bliss, and I felt alive again! I was like a little kid on Christmas—giddy and happier than I have ever felt before. Everything made sense to me. The Bible had always bored me and was difficult for me to understand. These books put teachings from the Bible in a simpler form that I understood. It was as if I had unlocked the magic key to life.

The Magic is a paperback book that I had set on my nightstand for quite some time. Because of my busy schedule, it was harder for me to physically read a book than it was for me to listen to one. In the meantime, I continued following Silvia on Instagram, seeing special things happen in her life that seemed to have a deeper meaning. Still, an inner feeling kept telling me to make the time to read.

I knew the book would be magical, so I listened to my inner guide. I knew if *The Magic* was half as good as Rhonda's first three books, then it would be worth my time. I told myself I would read one chapter a day. The chapters are short—only three to five pages—so I knew that was doable. The words were big, and the sentences were very simple to read, so it was my kind of book.

I started getting up thirty minutes earlier to read a chapter or two in the morning before I would start my day. Soon, though, I found myself being drawn back to read more throughout my day. The words were so simple, but yet so deep! I couldn't stop reading.

Gratitude

The Magic is about the power of gratitude. In the book are twenty-eight practices created to help people invite more gratitude into their lives. And the more gratitude there is, the greater the power a person has to make their silent desires and wildest dreams come into full bloom. This is regarding every aspect of our lives from our finances, our relationships, and our health.

The most influential people in history practiced gratitude and whose achievements put them amongst the greatest human beings who have ever lived: Jesus, Gandhi, Mother Teresa, St. Francis of Assisi, Martin Luther King Jr., the Dalai Lama, Buddha, Leonardo Da Vinci, Plato, Shakespeare, Lincoln, Einstein, and many, many more. And Jesus always said *thank you* first before he performed any miracle.

The scientists, philosophers, inventors, discoverers, and prophets who have practiced gratitude reaped its results, and most of them were aware of its inherent power. Yet, the power of gratitude is still unknown to the lives of most people today. To experience the magic of gratitude, you have to practice it. And the more you practice it, the better you become at it!

I began applying the teachings from *The Magic* to my life, and I soon realized how I had taken so many things for granted. Most times, without even realizing it. The teachings spoke to me with such clarity, that I became more open to the possibility of becoming an alchemist.

In ancient teachings, it is said that when a person reaches the point of being deeply grateful for the air that they breathe, their gratitude will have reached a new level of power. As a result, they will become an alchemist—one who can effortlessly turn every part of their life into gold.

I thought, *WOW! Is that really possible? That would be amazing.* If I didn't have to work as hard as I had during my first thirty-five years, but yet live a magical life with less effort, then that was worth a try to me. I had often wondered how certain people achieved amazing accomplishments in their lives, and from where their drive continued to come, because I was thirty-five years young and already burned out.

Over time, *Thank you* became the two most important words that I would say, think, write, and feel. I would wake, and give thanks for all the things that I loved in my life, and all the things that I desired like they already existed. I would write thank you on every receipt for every purchase I would make for business and personal.

At times, I would also randomly give money away. One time, my daughter caught me and said to me, "Mom, stop giving all of dad's money away."

"Sweetie," I said as I looked at her, "it is not dad's money; it is God's money, and He will always take care of us,"

This was not a concept that I had inherited; this was me choosing to live my life on pure faith. And when you get good at giving, I learned, is when abundance flows to you. As Eckhart Tolle once said, "If the only prayer you say in your whole life is 'thank you,' that would suffice."

Rhonda Byrne says it best in *The Magic:* "Gratitude is riches and complaint is poverty; it is the golden rule of your whole life, whether it is your health, job, relationships, or money. The more grateful you can be for the money you have, even if you do not have much, the more riches you will receive. And the more you complain about money, the poorer you will become."

Gratitude, I have realized, is about redirecting one's inner state from a scarcity mindset to one of plenty's. A story I learned from Sunday school as a child highlighted this: The Miracle of the Five Loaves and Two Fish. In this story, Jesus fed 5,000 men, plus women and children, from five barley loaves and two small fish. As children, we were taught this to show that Jesus always had enough.

That being said, we are meant to live a life of abundance! Often times, I had asked my husband, "What is the point of working, saving all your money for retirement, and then dying?" My inner guidance was not okay with this concept. I decided I was not going to follow the crowd, and that I would instead take the road less traveled. What I now know is that abundance and scarcity are both inner states that manifest as your reality!

Although this new way of life was better for me, I had actually been raised with a lack thereof mentality, which I never understood. However, I do not blame my parents for how they raised me. I was never handed anything, and for that reason, it shaped me and gave me a drive that I did not understand until now.

I would not be the person I am today if I had been raised differently; so with that being said, I am very grateful to my parents. Now, I know they were doing the best they knew how. They were not blessed with the resources that I have been blessed with. With all the technology today, we have unlimited knowledge at our fingertips.

For I know the plans I have for you, plans to prosper you and not to harm you, plans to give you hope and a future.

—JEREMIAH 29:11

🕊🕊🕊
The Most Important Thing

One day at the local dance boutique, I was in the middle of buying my daughter some dance tights. I always have my children sign the receipt for items that they are purchasing. My daughter checked out, and signed the receipt. She knows to always write *thank you* on them, however, she didn't write *thank you* this time.

"Makayla," I said, "you forgot the most important thing,"

"Mom, she's (the cashier lady) not going to see me write *thank you* on my receipt."

"It is not for her," I reminded. "It's for you to feel grateful that you have the fifty dollars to spend instead of thinking, 'Oh my goodness! I just spent fifty dollars on two pairs of tights.'"

Behind the counter, the lady who checked us out spoke up. "I like that.

I've never thought of it like that, or heard it put that way."

The more I practiced gratitude, the more it became who I am. I could feel gratitude soaking into my soul. Gratitude is more than a word—it is a feeling. Therefore, the ultimate aim in practicing gratitude is to deliberately *feel* it is much as you can, because it is the force of your feelings that accelerates the magic in your life. When you practice gratitude a little, your life will change a little. When you practice gratitude a lot, your life will change dramatically and in ways that you can hardly imagine. What I have grown to discover is that by giving thanks in everything, you penetrate the whole mystery of life, and you open up the gateway for an abundance of blessings. Ephesians 5:20 tells us, "To give thanks always for all things." And Matthew 5:8 further says, "Blessed are the pure in heart, for they shall see God."

I know it is hard to believe two words can have so much impact, but I have experienced their power first-hand.

The magic I was experiencing became my daily inspiration and my days became entirely spectacular. My kids would even ask me if I was *magic*. I thought that was really cute, but I did not take the credit. I told them, "I am a vessel that God is using for the greatest good for all." I was happier than I thought was possible here on Earth. I was blissfully happy—the happiest I have ever been. Gratitude was changing me, and my whole life was magically changing because of it.

> *As we express our gratitude, we must never forget that the highest appreciation is not to utter words, but to live by them.*
>
> —JOHN F. KENNEDY

To Believe in Miracles

In the meantime, I was led to another author that really resonated with me: Gabrielle Bernstein. Gabrielle Bernstein is the #1 New York Times bestselling author of *The Universe Has Your Back* and has written six additional bestsellers. She spends her time being a highly accomplished motivational speaker, life coach, and author who teaches primarily from the text, *A Course In Miracles.* Additionally, she is a certified Kundalini yoga and meditation teacher, as well as a student of Transcendental Meditation, taught by the David Lynch Foundation.

Firstly, I started reading *The Universe Has Your Back,* and then went onto her other works: *Super Attractor, Spirit Junkie, Miracles Now,* and *May Cause Miracles.* I happily finished all four of these books on Audible within a few weeks. In *The Universe Has Your Back,* Gabrielle talked about how she would ask for a sign when she needed to make a major decision, or needed clear direction in her life. Her sign was a butterfly. She encourages you to pick your own sign that means something to you.

As I pondered the thought of having my own sign and how awesome that would be if it actually worked, I went back to the verse, "In all your ways acknowledge him and he will direct your path" (Proverbs 3:6). I thought, *Wow! This could be a game-changer! What if this would work in my life?* My spirit told me to pick a white bird, and so I followed. I knew that white birds are used as a symbol of peace, and I knew I could use more peace in my life. To further help, I have daily reminders in my children's, my husband's, and in my phone that remind us to "believe in miracles," and to "choose love over fear." Gabrielle taught me this, and I try to instill these values within my family, and especially within my children.

Live Out the Example

Wayne Dyer has said that "our children have the anchor of the Universe located within them." This means that from the moment they are first conceived, they are gifted with their own inner guidance with which they will go through life. Lessons from the *Tao Te Ching* of Lao Tzu— considered one of the most highly treasured books of wisdom ever written —teaches us that "everything under Heaven is a sacred vessel and cannot be controlled. Trying to control leads to ruin." This encourages us to allow our lives to unfold naturally, and to also allow the lives of others to do the same. As we do, we are to take comfort in the fact that this is a good path, because we are all united under a divine plan.

As parents, our calling is to model unconditional love, led by example, and to protect our children to the best of our abilities. At the same time, however, we have to give them their own space to be.

Although they have come into this world through us, they are far from being our possessions. They are meant to make mistakes and experience human suffering, as we all do. We are not meant to spare them from heartache, sadness, or suffering; because it's through these things that one evolves. Eckhart Tolle tells us that the noble purpose of suffering "is to burn up the ego," as well as "to evolve the consciousness."

In order to influence another to the glorious nature of their own being, be a vibrational example. This includes being unafraid of unleashing your own magic, and instead, making the decision to radiate love. Give yourself permission to allow your own aura to radiate, and shine from within your own soul. When your vibration is raised, it affects people on a higher level. If you try to intervene, or force things onto another, expect there to be resistance. However, by being the glowing example, you become a bright energy field that opens others up to be receptive. In doing this, I try to live out the example I want to see within my children and in the world.

Additionally, I tell my children they can do and be anything that their heart desires, as long as they believe in themselves. When you believe in yourself, you are trusting in the wisdom that created you. I tell them that I believe in them and that they are the smartest, most talented, kindest, most beautiful, healthiest, wisest, most loving, most grateful and most magical creations that I know.

Speak to your children as if they are the wisest, kindest, most beautiful and magical humans on earth., for what they believe is what they will become.

—BROOKE HAMPTON

Vision Boards

My son was ten years old when I came to him with honesty. "Bud, mom is so grateful that you are athletic, but momma cannot keep going like this. I am not taking care of myself at this point, and that's not being of service to you, me, or the world. There are days that I don't even have time to shower; so something has to change. You are going to have to seek inward, and really ask yourself which sport you are most passionate about."

I knew that it takes ten thousand hours to become great at something, and if you want to be great, focus on what you are passionate about. You become an expert by devoting yourself to anything diligently for ten years.

While my son thought about what I had asked of him, my spirit told me to do vision boards with my children. This was towards the end of July, just before school and all the sports were about to start back full force. I had learned about vision boards in one of the books that I had listened to, and this concept spoke to my soul. With a new desire in my heart, I took my kids to our local coffee shop so they could feed off the good energy there. While we were inside, I had them write down several things: five things they are grateful for; five goals for the school year; and the one most important goal that would impact their life the most.

My son's goals consisted of the following: good handwriting; read; be nice; be smart; and have fun. He is grateful for his family; his life; his health; that he gets to go to school; that he gets to do sports; and that his family is blessed. His #1 goals are to be on tour, read more, and be a member in a golf community, so that he can work toward his long term goals.

My daughter's goals consisted of: getting all A's; reading at least three times a week; working on her typing skills on the Ratatype website; doing her best in everything she does; and to pay attention and focus. She is grateful for her family; that she gets to get a good education; that she lives in a beautiful home; that she has wonderful parents; and that her family is very blessed. Her #1 goal is to treat others the way she wants to be treated.

After the goal/gratitude sheets were complete, we went home and worked on the next part of their vision boards. We printed out pictures that they loved of the images that they held in their imagination. I told them that their imagination is their private venue; it is theirs and theirs alone that comes from Spirit. I let them know that anything that they imagine and hold in their imagination will eventually become their reality. As I've encouraged my children, I encourage you now: let your imagination go wild, and place no limits on what you can imagine for your life. Always stand strong in your faith, don't you ever doubt yourself, and always believe in your dreams, because they were given to you for a reason. Dream + Imagination= Success!

  To finish, I told my children to find every picture they could of all that they desired, and of how they imagine their lives to be. We then cut those out, and glued them on a decently-sized card stock sheet. I told them, then, to feel the feelings of gratitude from their heart of having their desires now, as if their desires were already a present fact. After that, we neatly displayed their completed vision boards within their rooms, in a place where they would see them every day. This all has its purpose, as creation originates in the world of spirit, and your imagination is the Source of all that has yet to manifest.

Imagination is everything. It is the preview of life's coming attractions.

—ALBERT EINSTEIN

Balance

My son had a few weeks of downtime, and we realized he didn't know what to do with his time unless he was busy playing a sport.

My husband Jason came home that afternoon, and told me, "I'm signing Kaiden back up for football."

"Nope," I replied firmly. "Not this time."

My husband seemed surprised. "Why do you get to pick?"

"I don't. He does. He is the only one that knows why he incarnated on this Earth, and what he came here to fulfill."

I showed my husband the vision boards that we had completed. I pointed out how there was nothing regarding football on them, except a picture of the new Falcons stadium that he wants to visit. We had worked hard on the vision boards, and I was not okay with them not serving their purpose.

"I cannot teach my son to dream, and then tell him that he is playing football instead."

My husband was unsure of how he felt about all of this. He needed some time to reflect, so we did not speak for twelve hours.

The next morning, however, he compromised: "I give you one year."

"That is all I ask for."

Over time, the vision boards truly did change our lives. And six months later, my husband's mind was changed when he told me, "I get it now...and thank you!" Kaiden had found his true passion, and was giving it his full focus. To be a golfer is all his heart desires, and for the first time in quite a long time, we had a balance in our lives again.

We now all keep ongoing vision boards and lists of our top desires. As we receive or accomplish desires, we cross them off the list, and add new ones as they come. Now, our ongoing lists consist of desires in the following areas:

- Our spiritual goals
- Our health and bodies
- Our life goals
- Our money
- Our relationships
- Our material desires
- Our magical to-do-list
- Places we want to travel
- Any areas we want improvement in

🕊🕊🕊
Intuition

As my son's birthday was coming up, he came to me, telling me that all he wanted was a dog for his birthday. My mother had been bitten in the face by a dog when she was five years old, and had to get two hundred and five stitches, which resulted in a lifelong scar. Needless to say, I was not raised with animals in my home, so I did not even know where to begin. To add on, I really didn't want anything else to take care of, since I had enough responsibilities already. In the meantime, I came across this quote by Robert Benchley that said: "Every boy needs two things: a dog, and a mother who lets him have one." This spoke to me so deeply, that I knew I had to grant my son his wish.

Before, though, I directed my attention back to Proverbs 3:6. This was a huge decision that would affect our lives for many years to come. I thanked God that he had given me clear direction on which breed of dog that would work best for our family, and asked Him to send me a white bird when the time was right.

Soon, I started doing my research and discussing dogs with others during random conversations. I knew we should start with a mid-size dog that was hypoallergenic, smart, low maintenance, and white in color. I did four months of research and searching. We had narrowed it down to a Westie or a Cavapoo.

A short time had passed before I had come across a lady who had a new litter of Westies. Out of the entire litter, only one had been left unchosen, still needing an owner. To see for ourselves, I gathered my kids in the car, and we drove out to the lady's home that afternoon. While my son was focused on the dog, I was searching everywhere for my white bird. I had just wanted to be done with this process already because I had so many other things to be focusing on; but still, there was no white bird to be found.

I heard my son happily tell me, "Mom, I really want this dog. He is so cute." The puppy still had three weeks before he would be ready to leave his mother, but the lady needed a deposit to hold the dog for me. My intuition told me, *NO*, but my son told me, "YES!" I began to doubt that the sign thing would even work for me, so I gave the lady the deposit. My kids were ecstatic.

As I drove home, I frantically read on my phone everything I saw regarding Westies. Minutes passed, and what started as a small pain in my stomach had grown into an uncomfortable knot. By the time I arrived home, I could barely speak. My entire stomach had tightened, and my breath had become too quick for me. I began to cry.

"Honey, what's wrong with you? I have never seen you act like this." My husband was confused when he saw me after my children and I had arrived home.

"I don't know," I answered. "But, I feel awful."

"If getting a dog is getting to you this much, then we should not get one."

"I have to contact the Westie breeder and tell her I am backing out. I don't even care if she keeps my deposit," I told him. I knew this was my intuition telling me *NO*, and I knew that I needed to honor it.

My family, however, grew really impatient with me. My kids even told me, "Mom, we're never going to get a dog, because you are so picky,"

"I have asked for a sign," I said. "And I really want to give it a little while longer to see if it really will work in my life." Still, they were beginning to think that I was crazy.

In ancient teachings, it is revealed that intuition is the knowledge that comes from a higher level of consciousness. Trust the intuition that your soul feels. Intuition is communication from our Source. It is a life skill that strengthens the more we use and rely on it. As you learn to trust your intuition, you will know it is one of your most powerful abilities.

❦❦❦
Sweet Boy

It was a Tuesday morning when I called my husband to tell him that I had found a really cute dog in California. "We can pay to ship him here and he could be here by next week," I said.

"That is crazy, and we are not doing that," he said.

"Fine, then we will continue to wait."

Hours later, around noon, I received an excited call from my husband. "Honey, get online! I just had an alert come through from a local breeder that just received a new litter of Cavapoos, and we could go out there this afternoon."

I went online and looked at the picture of the litter. There was one white puppy that was back in the corner all by himself. "He's cute and all, but there is still no white bird."

"Honey, I am telling you that he is the one," my husband insisted.

I knew in my heart that this was the day. When I ended the phone call from my husband, I said a quick prayer that went something like: "God, this is it. My family has grown impatient with me, so I have to make a decision today and I really want to know this sign thing works in my life too. Could you please send a white bird today?"

When my daughter and I pulled in our driveway that afternoon, we drove up to a picture of a white bird that my husband had taped to the garage door. Makayla and I started laughing so hard that we had tears running down our faces. It was one of the cutest things that my husband has ever done.

I walked inside our house and called out to my husband. "That is cute and all, but that does not count."

He was undeterred. "Let's just get in the car and see what happens."

I agreed, so we headed out. We were about five minutes out from our destination when my husband started tapping me harder and harder. "Honey, honey, honey... do you see that?"

I looked up from my phone and watched one white bird fly across the interstate, right in front of our car. My husband about had an accident from his excitement. I knew that I had read that a sign would be crystal clear, one that I could not deny nor have to question. But, this experience was more magical than what I could have ever imagined. I didn't even know actual white birds existed in Georgia. When I asked for a white bird, I was thinking I would see one in the form of a statue, or on a billboard, or something like that.

I cried, and said to my family, "We are getting this dog,"

We were in amazement at what had just happened. We arrived at the local pet store named Puppies From Heaven, we knew without any hesitation that this little white Cavapoo would be coming home with us as a new addition to our family.

As we were driving home with our new fur baby, I asked my husband, "What if we name him after your father?"

He paused for a bit before he finally answered. "That is a lovely idea!"

My husband hadn't talked much about his father in the fourteen years since he had passed, so I knew it could be a good way for him to reconnect with his father. This is how Benny got his name. A precious thing I have noticed is that Benny and my husband have a connection and bond that is unexplainable. There are often times my husband will tell me that Benny is his dad reincarnated.

To add on, Benny, or our "Sweet Boy," has been more than a blessing to our family. He has been the missing piece that we didn't even know that we were missing. I see why it has been said that "a dog is a man's best friend." He is our little shadow—always right by our side. He has brought laughter, unity within the family, and has shown us a true example of divine love. All in all, Benny is the smartest, submissive, most obedient little angel; and we feel very strongly that he was sent directly to us from Heaven. I had no idea such a creature existed. To this day, we are beyond grateful that he is our angel.

Lifelong Messenger

My spirit told me to dig deeper into the meaning behind the white bird. In summary, this is what I found: white doves are symbols used by many cultures around the world. It is for this reason that they are regarded as symbols, usually of peace, of love, or of messengers. Their symbolism can be found anywhere in major and minor religious groups, as well as in groups promoting both war and peace. Upon learning this, I was in awe! I know now why I had chosen a white bird as my sign. And I was overjoyed to know that I would have a lifelong messenger when seeking guidance.

Eckhart Tolle touches on this in his book, *A New Earth*. In it, he says: "When you are alert and contemplate a flower, crystal, or bird without naming it mentally, it becomes a window to you in the formless. There is an inner opening, however slight, into the realm of spirit.

This is why these three 'enlightened' life-forms have played such an important part in the evolution of human consciousness since ancient times; why, for example, the jewel in the lotus flower is a central symbol of Buddhism, and a white bird, the dove, signifies the Holy Spirit in Christianity. They have been preparing the ground for a more profound shift in planetary consciousness that is destined to take place in the human species. This is the spiritual awakening that we are beginning to witness now."

A few months later, I was headed out to a printing company to which I was referred by our branding specialist. This printing company would be printing over ten thousand dollars worth of new stationery for our company, so this was kind of a big deal. On my way out to the printing company, I prayed a short prayer: "God, it will be really cool if I get here today, and there are white birds."

A short while later, as I pulled up to the building, my husband Facetimed me. "Honey, you are not going to believe this," I told him excitedly.

"What is it?" he asked.

"I don't even have to look for the building sign. There are white birds everywhere."

I showed him what I was looking at, and I shared with him the little prayer that I had prayed. We both were in awe. I, of course, I had to take a picture; it was one of the prettiest things that I had ever seen. Once I had gotten out of my car and walked inside, I had complete peace that I was in the right place. Needless to say, this printing company was a true gift, and Kip, one of the owners, will be a lifelong friend. I cried all the way home that day. To experience such peace here on Earth is the coolest thing I have ever experienced. I could not believe life could be this magical.

People who wait for a magic wand fail to see that they ARE the magic wand.

—THOMAS LEONARD

The Choice to Stand in Faith

A few weeks later, I told my husband that I was feeling a strong pull to share my experiences with the world. With my Instagram rapidly growing, I knew I could use it as a platform to share things that were happening in my life, and to help others experience these things in their own lives. I told him that I would be asking for the white bird again, and later on, I began my prayer:

"God, if this is what you want me to do, then send me a white bird. And, you're going to have to make this easy for me, because I did not have time for it to be hard."

And, of course, on the next day, while I was at a golf course with my son, one white bird flew right behind him and my husband.

As a tear ran down my face, I made the choice to stand in my faith. "Okay, here we go!"

The next day, I Googled *how do I know if I am being guided,* and this is what I found: "If God is calling you to take a leap of faith, be encouraged by His presence." With this, I also found the following verses that spoke to my heart: "Have I not commanded you? Be strong and courageous. Do not be terrified, do not be discouraged, for the Lord your God will be with you wherever you go" (Joshua 1:9). And remember, "Cast all your anxiety on Him because He cares for you" (1 Peter 5:7). "Trust in the Lord with all your heart and lean not on your own understanding; in all your ways acknowledge Him, And He will direct your paths" (Proverbs 3: 5-6). So the journey began! I had complete peace that this was I was supposed to do.

Your bravery wins battles you cannot see. Your bravery strengthens others to win their battles, too.

—ANN VOSKAMP

Part Three: The Journey

Our Bodies, Our Temples

My daughter was diagnosed with ADD when she was seven years old, so that is where my love for health came into play. I have studied food and how it affects the brain and the rest of our body for the past eight years. I have grown to firmly believe that our greatest wealth is health. I was once asked why I care so much about what I put in my body because we are all going to die of something one day. My response to that was, "Yes, that is true, but for me, it is about the quality of life that I can live while I am here."

Our brains are the most powerful part of our bodies. They control everything we do from our actions, our decisions, our moods, and our behavior. What we put in our bodies feed our brains and our guts (our second brains). Since the brain is unseen, it is the most neglected by most people. Our bodies are temples, getting us through this life.

When we do not take care of our mind, body, and soul, it causes us pain and suffering.

Genesis 9:3 says, "Every moving thing that lives shall be food for you. And as I gave you the green plants, I give you everything." Additionally, Leviticus 11:1-7 says, "And the Lord spoke to Moses and Aaron, saying to them, 'Speak to the people of Israel, saying, These are the living things which you may eat among all the animals that are on earth. Whatever parts the hoof and is cloven-footed and chews the cud, among the animals, you may eat. Nevertheless, among those that chew the cud or part the hoof, you shall not eat these: The camel, because it chews the cud but does not part the hoof, is unclean to you. And the rock badger, because it chews the cud but does not part the hoof, is unclean to you. And the pig, because it parts the hoof and is cloven-footed but does not chew the cud, is unclean to you."

God told us what to eat. It is man-made processed foods that are making us so sick. "Do you not know that you are God's temple and that God's Spirit dwells in you? If anyone destroys God's temple, God will destroy him. For God's temple is holy, and you are that temple" (1 Corinthians 3:16-17). "For anyone who eats and drinks without discerning the body eats and drinks judgment on himself" (1 Corinthians 11:29). 1 Corinthians 10:31 says, "So, whether you eat or drink, or whatever you do, do all to the glory of God." I have experienced first-hand the healing that comes from food that we put in our body.

Let food be thy medicine and medicine be thy food.

—HIPPOCRATES

The Magic of Asheville

I do know that the study of food is part of my life purpose, so I knew I wanted to incorporate food on my Instagram page. I also knew I wanted to show support to the businesses at which I shop and eat because I know half the battle is knowing what and where to eat.

In the meantime, I had been told by a few different friends that knew my love for holistic care that I needed to visit Asheville, NC. Spring break for my children was approaching and Asheville kept coming up in conversations. After a while, I could not get the city off my mind; it was pulling at me like a magnetic pull. I made a few phone calls, did a bit of research, and then booked a last-minute trip Asheville. Soon after, I loaded up my kids, and we were off. Beforehand, I had made a few of my own plans, including visiting local healthy restaurants and posting about them on Instagram.

We were disappointed in our first few stops, so I was a bit confused on why I was pulled to come here, so I went back to the verse, "In all your ways acknowledge him and he will direct your path" (Proverbs 3:6). The next day, I dropped my son off at the local golf course, and my daughter and I headed downtown. I started asking the locals what they recommended for us to do. I was led from one place to the next.

My favorite stop was a little shop called Earth Magick. The name obviously spoke to me, but I knew there was something deeper that I had to discover. As I went to the front counter, I asked the lady if there were any must-haves in her store that I needed to take home with me. She then led me over to a small section of the store, and she tells me that every woman needs this chocolate "Moon Cycle" ghee. I immediately knew this was the answer to my prayers. I had asked God to take my sugar desire away from me because I knew it no longer served me. I happily purchased a few jars.

Ghee traces its roots to the ancient traditions of Ayurveda, a system of medicine with historical roots in the Indian subcontinent, which really intrigues me. It deals with matters relating to health, day to day life and longevity (long life). The Chopra Center describes Ayurveda as "a science of life (Ayur = life, Veda = knowledge or wisdom). More than a mere system of treating illness, it offers a body of wisdom designed to help people stay vibrant and healthy while realizing their full human potential. The two main guiding principles of Ayurveda are: the mind and the body are inextricably connected, and nothing has more power to heal and transform the body than the mind. Ayurveda is the oldest form of natural medicine and lifestyle system. It involves balancing elements on the inside of our bodies and mind to foster optimal health and maintenance."

The Chopra Center also provides a few Ayurvedic practices that may strengthen your digestion, thus helping your gut (second brain) in functioning to its best ability:

- Always sit down to eat (don't eat in front of your computer, TV, while on your phone, or while driving).
- Don't wait to eat until you are definitely hungry.
- Eat at a moderate pace. Don't inhale your food or eat too slowly.
- Drink hot water with ginger throughout your day.
- Practice some form of moderate exercise on a regular basis.
- Spend time in the quiet of meditation every day.
- Use detoxifying herbs such as triphia, ashwagandha, guggulu, brahmi, ginger, turmeric, and neem.
- According to Ayurveda, sleep is the nursemaid to humanity. Our bodies repair and rejuvenate during sleep. A lack of sleep disrupts the

body's innate balance, weakens our immune system, and speeds up the aging process.

Additionally, ghee is considered nourishment of holy, restorative, and purifying means. The "Moon Cycle" ghee is an herbal blend that supports hormone balancing and emotional support. I cannot speak highly enough about the results I get from my daily dose of "Moon Cycle" chocolate ghee. It did break me from my sugar cravings, but more than that, I no longer get cramps or mood swings from hormones, which is true magic!

I purchased the ghee and the elixir syrups both from the Earth Magick store. Both of these were made from the same company, Goddess Ghee, which you can find on Google or Amazon. Elixir syrups are a holistic approach that helps promote natural overall wellness. The "open heart elixir" is a traditional oxymel syrup with herbs for uplifting the heart. It is infused with fresh tulsi, rose petals, and schizandra berries. Oxymel syrup was designed specifically for individuals dealing with conditions of the mind. Tulsi, or Holy Basil, is "Queen of Herbs," and is one of the most sacred plants in India. The "garden of the goddess elixir" is also an oxymel that is infused with fresh garden herbs consisting of rosemary, sage, thyme, lavender, and mint. The "elderberry elixir" is most commonly taken during cold and flu season. It is a natural soothing relief for seasonal distress. I like to add these syrups in decaffeinated herbal hot teas, or drink straight from the spoon. These three elixirs became staple pieces in my home.

Embellish was another little shop that I know I was led to while I was in Asheville. Barb is the owner, and we had an immediate connection. Once inside, I could feel the love and passion she held for her shop. The air was filled with heavenly lingering aromas, and the treasures there were all authentic, special gifts. I am a sucker for finding gifts that have a deeper lasting impression. I purchased treasures from her that I have absolutely loved so much, that I have placed several more orders from her that I have given as gifts to others.

Leaving Asheville was bittersweet. Asheville is known for being dubbed "Paris of the South." It is a center for holistic healing, thanks to the native Cherokee tribe. Nearly 80% of all plant species used in North American herbalism is native there. I traveled there not knowing why, and left there knowing the people and things that I was led to could only be described as divine guidance and alignments. The energy that was rushing through my body was like nothing I have ever felt. I felt more alive than ever! I realized at thirty-five that I am a wanderlust, and it all made sense to me now. I never liked being on a time clock; I love to live in the moment.

My prayer each day became, "Thank you, God, that you have strengthened my knowledge, my insights, my intuition, my wisdom, my love, my gratitude, my abilities, my creativity, my clarity, and understanding. Thank you for thinking through me, speaking through me, working through me and loving though me. Thank you for leading me to where you want me to go, for giving me the words to say, and to whom." This has made all the difference in the world! The power of prayer is unbelievable, and just pure magic.

A good traveler has no fixed plans, and is not intent on arriving.

—LAO TZU

The Meaning of Melissa

As time went on, I was led to one thing after the next, and my Instagram page began to capture all my focus. I realized that I wanted to share the magic of life with the world, and after about three months, my page was really starting to come together. I read a blog post one morning regarding name meanings, and my spirit said, *Melissa, Google your name.*

What I had found went like this: "In ancient mythology, *Melissa* is a 'Queen Bee Goddess,' looking after all women. She is a strong, confident female who possesses great leadership skills. Usually popular, *Melissa* creates the strongest of bonds with only a select few who she deems worth her time. And her time is precious indeed. With her stunning beauty and singing voice, *Melissa* knows how to captivate her audience. *Melissa* is a true friend and a passionate lover. She is loyal to the end.

With her passion and ambition, a *Melissa* can do anything she puts her mind to.

"The honey bee is an insect that feeds on pollen, nectar, and honey, and stores them in the hive. Female bees do all the work of nest making and provisioning. Most bees gather pollen from a wide variety of flowers. God sends *Melissa* out in search of those who need His help in their lives, and to gather the resources needed to help them. *Melissa,* like the bee, is a tireless worker. She gathers information from many resources, never trusting just one source for the accuracy she needs. *Melissa* is never satisfied until she has searched for what it is she needs to know. She then stores all this in her heart, not just in her head.

"It may seem that *Melissa* is nosey, but it is much more than just being nosey. She has a need to know things because she uses the information she gathers to gain insight into situations that need her attention. There are those who need *Melissa* to know what is in their hearts, for it is nearly impossible for them to say these things aloud. These are the ones to whom God sends *Melissa*. She has a way of finding out these things and with God's help, is nearly always able to provide the needed help."

I immediately called my mom after reading what I had found. "Mom, why did you name me Melissa? Could you not have named me something else?"

She did not have a clear explanation. I sent her what I had found, and we both could not believe what we were reading. I cried, again! I finally knew why I was such a seeker, and why I was wired the way that I am. My name fits me perfectly!

After reading this, I returned to my Instagram page and scrolled through. I observed how my entire page was green, white, and earth-toned. To my surprise, I had been choosing colors that were healing to me, without even knowing the meaning behind my name. I found this super fascinating.

We all have certain colors to which we are drawn, and all colors have meanings. They evoke feelings and emotions, and likewise, we tend to choose colors that reflect our moods and desires. The ones on our clothing, in our interior designs, and on our cars, for example, all reflect how we feel about ourselves.

According to the Universe of Symbolism, colors "have profound spiritual meanings, and can greatly affect our vibrations, and even how others perceive us." The following are the colors to which I feel the most drawn, and how the Universe of Symbolism defines them:

- White symbolizes innocence, purity, faith, and peace. It represents cleanliness, reverence, and humility.
- Green is the color of nature and the environment. The symbolism is health, youth, renewal, and good luck. It is used for overall healing and renewal.

- Blue is the color of cool water and the sky. It is soothing and symbolically represents trust and harmony; it also holds the energy and meaning of calm.
- Gray represents good taste; a touch of formality lending to dignity and self-respect.
- Brown is the color of the earth. It represents all organic matter and fertile grounds. Brown represents planting new seeds and a connection to Gaia or earth. Earth is a natural healer bringing inner peace, and decreasing depression.

Positive Thoughts & Expectations

My husband came to me one day saying, "I need to take two weeks off work,"

"Then, take two weeks off," I replied. 'What's going on?"

He looked me deep into my eyes. "I want to experience the things you are experiencing because that is life, but I know if I were to take time off, our business would fall apart."

This brought tears to my eyes once again. My husband expressed to me that he had even grown a bit envious of me. This was one of my biggest fears. I knew I was evolving so much spiritually, that it did concern me a bit that we would not understand each other anymore. As he was bogged down with the day to day responsibilities of our company, he allowed me to engulf myself with podcast after podcast, book after book, with no questions asked. I am forever grateful to my husband for allowing me to rediscover myself. He has never questioned me on what I was doing, or how I was spending my time or money. Of course, I never gave him a reason to ask.

     I knew that worrying is asking the universe to give you exactly what you don't want, and thoughts become reality whether they are good, or whether they are bad. Therefore, I ensure that I only hold positive thoughts and expectations about life. I prayed, saying "Thank you God that you have sent my husband help, so that he can have the time to start to experience your grace in his own life. And Thank you God that you have sent me like-minded women on the same path as me." I was putting into practice what I had learned: that we should give thanks that we have already received what we desire as if we have already received it.

     A few weeks later, I received a phone call from my husband. "Honey, what have you been praying for?"

"I thanked God that he has sent you help," I replied.

"Honey," he continued, "my phone is ringing off the hook, and not just by people, but by amazing people. Whatever you are doing, keep doing it, because it is working, and I can feel it!"

As a man thinketh in his heart, so shall he be.

—PROVERBS 23:7

Moai Angel Sisters

The next morning, I went on Instagram while on the way back from my 4:30 am gym session with my husband. I saw a post from a local yoga instructor, and I immediately had a sense come over me that was so strong. I looked at my husband and said, "I have to go to yoga today and I am not sure why."

I have never liked organized gym classes, but I knew my intuition was pulling me there for a reason that I could not ignore. When I walked in, guess who was there? Silvia from Good Tidings! Once again, our lives intertwined. I now practice yoga at least five days a week, and I have been blessed with friends that I didn't know existed in this lifetime; the most amazing friends a girl could ask for.

As I continued going, I got involved in a group chat between Silvia, Tammie (the yoga instructor), and two other women, Ragin and Caurie. I have no idea how it all was orchestrated, but I now know it was all divine! We each have our own thing going on: Silvia has her Good Tidings company (www.goodtidingsstyle.com); Tammie is a yoga instructor, and health and wellness coach (www.blissfullysoulful.com); Ragin is the founder of a non-profit named Radiant Faces; and Caurie is the founder of Lavender (https://feelthelav.com).

With this group chat, we started sharing inspirational things and podcasts several times a week. After a few weeks, we decided to meet up and have a formal outing as the five of us, deciding on dinner at Del Frisco's in Atlanta. While we were there, a man came up to us, telling us that he is a messenger. His energy froze us; it was as if the whole world had stopped moving! He went on to tell us that we are "a Moai group that will be lifelong friends!" He continued on, stating that he had "the strongest pull to come into Del Frisco's and he wasn't sure why." He ordered nothing, but instead paid for our entire bill, and then was gone in a flash. The encounter gave us all chills and left us all on a high that we had never felt before. We all knew it could only be explained as a divine encounter that would impact us forever, and that would never be forgotten!

Similarly, we call ourselves "Moai Angel Sisters." According to Wellness Multiplied, Moais are a supportive group of wellness warriors that become lifelong friends that make the wellness journey more fun, successful, and rewarding. Traditionally, they are a group of five people that originally join as a social support group, and form in order to provide support, whether it be of a financial, health, or spiritual interest. Moai means "meeting for a common purpose" in Japanese, and originated from the social support groups in Okinawa, Japan. These groups are highly believed to be one of the primary causes of a long and prosperous life among the Okinawan people, which in turn causes this area to have one of the highest concentrations of centenarians anywhere. Moais are considered one of the leading factors of living extraordinarily better and longer lives than almost anyone in the world.

Just like the Moai are like a family, these incredible women have become my family. We encourage, appreciate, support, respect, and inspire one another on a deeper level. These women inspire me to be a better wife, mother, friend, daughter, aunt; an overall better version of myself, each and every day. We share books, podcasts, insights, laughter, love, and advice, as well as a bunch of other things: recipes, fashion tips, parenting insights, life skills, inspiration, health and wellness tips, and spiritual guidance.

We each bring the missing piece of the puzzle that makes the life circle whole. We each sharpen each other in areas that need to be sharpened, and we push and encourage each other beyond our own comfort zones. We collaborate and come together as a team when one of us is in need, or if one of our family members is in trouble. We don't hesitate to pick each other up and to speak life over one another. We have now come to believe that our souls joined many years ago, looked at the Earth and decided that we would together elevate one another and the consciousness of the planet. This would be to help others live Heaven on Earth, on Earth as it is in Heaven. It is much easier to go through life knowing there is a safety net with such love and support!

Research shows that your social connections have a long-term impact on your health and happiness. You mimic the habits of your three closest friends. If you share similar values, health habits, and life goals, then you are likely to experience less stress, be happier, and live longer. Loneliness can decrease your life expectancy by fifteen years. With each happy friend you add to your network, you increase your happiness by fifteen percent, and happiness has a beautiful tendency of being contagious. By finding the right tribe, you will add years to your life, as well as enjoy your time here a lot more.

Never doubt a small group of thoughtful committed people can change the world. Indeed, it is the only thing that ever has.

—MARGARET MEAD

*Part Four:
Turning Within*

Union

A few weeks into my yoga practice, I started to experience epiphanies and *AHA!* moments quite frequently. I was piecing life together on a deeper level. I knew I was really enjoying yoga, but I also knew there was something more that I was also gaining. I started to do a bit of research into the benefits of yoga, and this is what I discovered:

"Yoga means "union," and to completely know yourself and to be at peace in yourself. It integrates the mind, body, and spirit. You connect with your soul which enables you to discover your soul purpose. You gain a clear knowledge of the oneness of yourself with the source of all life. It is a peace that is freedom from suffering, doubt, and confusion. A natural blessedness unfolds in you as you feel this peace, and you increasingly realize this is the core essence of who you are. Being established in this knowledge, your life starts to flow with a vital freshness and harmony, with clarity, mental alertness and a fullness of a loving understanding."

One day, I was led to a podcast by Dr. Bruce Lipton on the science of yoga, and after listening, things made even more sense. Dr. Lipton explained that yoga scientifically has the capacity to change your brain. It changes your neurology, nervous system, and physiology. There are studies that show that a major neurotransmitter is affected after a single yoga practice. There are other studies, as well, that show that the expression of our DNA and the activity of our genes are actually changed with each practice.

Yoga has proven itself over tens of thousands of years with a whole host of amazing benefits: improving focus, mindfulness, posture, breathing, flexibility, and sense of oneness; decreasing anxiety, depression, stress levels, and blood pressure; and elevating one's overall psychological well-being.

Moreover, it strengthens the power of the mind; and the more power we have over our minds, the more control we have in our lives.

Practicing yoga has been a gift to me, and has caused my mind and body to feel incredible. I know people may have their own opinions, but this is what I can attest to: yoga is not just a hobby, nor is it only reserved for certain types of people. It is the practice of unifying one with oneself, which gives birth to real biological and spiritual results. I stand firm in my belief that yoga is for absolutely anybody, and everybody is worthy of its powers to heal and restore.

Yoga doesn't just change the way we see things, it transforms the person who sees.

—B.K.S. IYENGAR

Muladhara

When learning about yoga, one also learns about chakras. We each have twelve chakras, or energy centers. The internal seven are the core energy centers that most people are aware of run down the body's midline from the base of the spine to the top of the head. The other five are located outside of our bodies. The *Earth Star Chakra* is located a foot and a half below our feet, and is responsible for our connection to the earth which can only be activated through meditation. The remaining four chakras: The *Soul Star Chakra*, the *Universal Chakra,* the *Galactic Chakra,* and the *Divine Gateway Chakra* are located just above our head which connects us to the higher Universal flow of energy.

Chakras connect our spiritual bodies to our physical bodies; and they also hold the key to creating harmony and a deeper connection amongst our body, mind, and spirit. For this reason, yoga and meditation are the most powerful tools we can use to open our chakras, and to obtain a more peaceful state of awareness and being. The following is the knowledge that I have gained through my own search for the meaning behind these chakras:

The seven major chakras are connected to different glands and organs within the body, and are responsible for the equal distribution of Parana, or life energy. Each chakra controls specific behaviors and values in our lives, such as material security, communication, and love. Yoga balances each chakra by creating alignment in the physical body. By balancing the chakras, you can receive clarity, peace, and fulfillment. You can also control specific behaviors, and overcome old patterns, beliefs, and habits. Practicing yoga clears and revitalizes the chakras, and allows prana to flow freely. When there is a disturbance in this life energy, or a blockage in any one or more chakras, then you also will experience a disturbance, as well, in either the physical, mental, or emotional sense.

Once you are aware of the chakras and each of their colors, you can begin to go about ways of awakening and strengthening them in order to balance all areas of your life. The chakra colors follow the spectrum of the rainbow. By balancing each one, you will have a better chance of staying mentally and physically fit, and also improve your financial and professional lives.

The first chakra is the base or root chakra, also known by its original name of Muladhara. It is located at the base of the spine, and is the root to our whole body and mind. It connects to our foundations and basic needs. Things that can unbalance this chakra can include: lack of security, financial instability, issues with survival, a nomadic life, or disconnection to one's family.

Connecting to the earth is a quick way to bring the root chakra into balance. The key to your root chakra is just that: to root. Walking barefoot in soil, sand, or grass from time to time will help to keep it in balance. When the root chakra is open and free from any blockages you will be assessing the most grounding and stabilizing energy, and the others will naturally flow.

You will feel very rooted and confident. You will feel stronger in your body and in your mind. All of the organs that make up your natural waste removal system are influenced by this chakra. Therefore, this chakra promotes good digestive health. It brings about a natural detox and cleansing energy that leaves you feeling fresh and healthy. An open root chakra also helps you to cope with cravings; and in turn, you tend to be less hungry, feel better balanced, and become more mindful with your overall eating patterns and your diet.

The color red is associated with our root chakra. Foods from the Earth that are healing to your root chakra are as follows: red apples, pomegranate, watermelon, cherries, and berries. Foods grown with roots or on a vine such as radishes, beets, parsnips, red beans, and lentils are also helpful. Red herbal teas such as rooibos or hibiscus; earthly mineral stews and broths; and animal proteins like red meat and eggs are all foods that are healing to your base chakra.

I am affirmations: *I am rooted. I am grounded. I am safe. I am secure.*

Svadhisthana

The second chakra is the sacral chakra, or Svadhisthana. It is located in the lower abdomen about two inches below the navel, or belly button. It is associated with feelings and emotions, and the expression of other good things: freedom, mercy, forgiveness, justice, transcendence, alchemy, diplomacy, intuition, prophecy, and revelation. This chakra is all about connecting to others and accepting change. It also relates to our ability to feel creative, sexual, and passionate.

When your second chakra is in balance, you experience the freedom to embody all God intends to give you. This chakra is the point where you make contact with your soul and receive guidance. Your soul is wise and gives you direction and intuition while you are on your own glorious path.

The color orange is associated with our sacral chakra. Foods like carrots, peppers, squash, oranges, tangerines, mangoes, passion fruit, honey, along with nuts, flax and sunflower seeds are its healing foods. This is in addition to others, such as: those with a high water element in them, cumin, turmeric, fennel, sesame seeds, ginger, mint, trace minerals, and teas that soothe and balance hormones. The sacral chakra also affects your sense of taste. By balancing it, you will benefit from a healthy weight loss and control over your senses. You become more selective with how you are nourished, focusing on quality foods over quantity.

I am affirmations: *I am healthy. I am creative. I am abundant. I am calm. I am intuitive.*

Manipura

The third is the solar plexus chakra, or Manipura. The solar plexus chakra is the energy center responsible for maintaining our health. It is located in the upper abdomen, just below the organ of the stomach. It influences the ability of our bodies to digest and eliminate, as well as influences the confidence of oneself. If there is too much of its energy, you may tend to feel like you need to show off, or control others. If this energy is blocked, however, you may feel insecure with yourself.

By opening and maintaining your third chakra, you can help to maintain a healthy and strong digestion, which can promote healing in your gut. A healthy digestion is immensely important because it is responsible for maintaining our overall health. Our gut is considered our second brain, which strongly influences our mood, affects our metabolism, and our immune system. It is the most important chakra with regards to ensuring that our physical health is operating well and at the highest strength.

The color yellow is associated with our solar plexus chakra. Activities such as dancing, and eating foods such as kefir, sauerkraut, Ceylon cinnamon, lemon, melons, bananas, aloe juice, avocado, fennel, and mint all benefit it. Yellow vegetables with high water base such as celery and cucumber, and herbal tea like peppermint and soothing chamomile are also healing to this third chakra.

I am affirmations: *I am worthy. I am strong. I am powerful. I am confident.*

Anahata

The fourth chakra is the heart chakra, or Anahata. It relates to how we process emotion and show love. This chakra sits at the center of our whole being, controlling our very existence. It is the center of love and devotion, kindness and compassion, giving and forgiving. From this center, we have the power to touch anyone. With its energy, we have the knowledge to self-heal and to heal others in both the physical and mental sense.

A blocked heart chakra can exhibit some of the following symptoms: defensiveness, controlling actions, suspiciousness, withdrawal, possessiveness, and fear of letting go. When in balance, however, an open heart chakra shows acceptance to others, to life, and to oneself.

This chakra also affects our largest organ: our skin. It is little wonder, then, that by opening the heart chakra and welcoming more love into your life, your skin will become clearer, firmer, and overall healthier.

To balance this chakra, get out in nature, learn to let go of anything that does not serve you, and instead, welcome in a loving life by practicing self-love, unconditional love to others, and gratitude.

The color green is associated with our heart chakra. Vibrant green nutrient-rich vegetables, such as: spinach, kale, dandelion greens, broccoli, and cabbage; green water-based alkalizing fruits and vegetables like green apples, zucchinis, and celery; water and green teas; healthy fats from raw nuts, avocado, green beans, lima beans, and mung beans; and herbs like basil, thyme, and cilantro are all healing foods for your heart chakra.

I am affirmation: *I am love. I am joy. I am compassionate. I am open. I am grateful.*

Vishuddhi

The fifth chakra is the throat chakra, or Vishuddhi. Our throat chakra is out of balance when we are not honoring, or speaking our truth. When your throat chakra is in balance, you are communicating more openly and fearlessly. With greater clarity in speech also comes better self-expression.

Throat chakra healing results in the healing of your thyroid, which in turn controls your metabolism. Healing of this chakra also helps you in becoming a better listener, as well as an appreciator of silence. This brings forth a great sense of peace that can be calming to the mind.

The color blue is the color associated with this chakra. Eating nutritional whole foods from the earth, such as: blueberries, blackberries, raspberries; and drinking wine, clear liquids or broths, herbal teas, alkaline or mineral water are all healing for our fifth chakra. Being in, or near the water; walking outside under the blue sky; and breathing in the fresh air are all things we can do to help regulate this chakra, as well.

I am affirmations: *I am letting go. I am balanced. I am truthful. I am liberated. I am a good listener.*

Ajna

The sixth is the third-eye chakra, or Ajna. The third-eye chakra is the eye of the soul. It represents intuition and the ability to see beyond what lies on the surface. It is also the gateway to the mind and intellect. Located between the eyebrows, the third-eye is said to be blocked when you feel intense anxiety or worry about the future. The third-eye chakra can take you out of your thinking brain, though, and into much lighter and higher places.

Opening this chakra gives you a sense of oneness with both humankind and the universe, increased synchronicity, and ease with psychic abilities, or hearing and seeing more than meets the eye. It helps you to live more in the present moment, as well as have a more refined and singular focus. It will also cause you to become less distracted, living more in each moment and opening you up to a higher consciousness.

When your third eye is blocked, you may experience fear of success, poor communication, and an inability to understand, which can all cause you to set your sights and standards low. By opening the third-eye chakra, you can attune your intuition and can gain a clearer understanding of your life's purpose. This will provide you with strength, determination, and a desire to succeed. Opening this chakra also helps you to open all the other chakras more easily, and it has been said that clearing your third-eye chakra releases your soul.

Indigo is associated with our third-eye chakra. Supported foods are: water; raw nuts especially walnuts; sprouted nuts especially almonds; mushrooms, goji berries, acai, plums, eggplant; cruciferous vegetables especially broccoli; clean organic meats; freshwater fish; and pineapple and papaya.

I am affirmations: *I am guided. I am centered. I am clear. I am intuitive. I am in the gap. I am divine consciousness. I am free from any blockages. I am present. I am oneness.*

Sahasrara

The seventh is the crown chakra, or Sahasrara. It is located at the top of the head, and it is your gateway to higher consciousness. The seventh chakra can only be experienced with the soul, and not the mind. When you truly open this chakra, your eyes will turn inward. Opening this chakra leads to self-realization.

The colors purple or white are associated with our crown chakra. Water, purified or salt, absorbed through the skin or top of the head; cleansing herbs; various seeds like chia and sesame; and bone and vegetable broths are all supportive of this chakra.

Our crown chakra is more spirit than Earth, so its nourishment really comes from sources other than food, including love and a strong connection to the Divine. Incense and smudging herbs like sage, copal, myrrh, frankincense, and juniper are all helpful. Fasting, detoxifying, meditation and positive thinking are also said to be beneficial for the crown chakra.

I am affirmations: *I am present. I am connected. I am here. I am being. I am positive. I am divine love.*

Chakra alignment, I have learned, affects us on a physical, spiritual, and mental level. On a physical level, we feel good and become healed when our energy is flowing freely. On a mental level, we become abundantly creative. On a spiritual level, we become more intuitive and enlightened. In the lower chakras, we can receive intense inspiration and excitement, but in the higher chakras, we turn inspiration into insight and awakenings.

Everything we do either disrupts or benefits our chakras in some way. This is why it is important to be mindful of what we are exposing ourselves and our five senses. Natural sunlight is essential for our chakra health, and even twenty minutes a day in the sun is sufficient. Vitamin D, produced by the body when it is regularly exposed to sunlight, promotes stronger bones and healthier bodily systems. The sun also plays a big role in determining if our chakras are open or closed.

The controlling of noise pollution is another essential part of maintaining chakra health. Noise pollution dilutes our sense of hearing, which, in turn, makes it difficult to open up our higher chakras. Our ears are the balance centers of our body, and if we constantly expose ourselves to unnatural noise, the chakras will not operate properly. This can lead to one feeling a sense of not being in control and feeling lost.

What we eat and drink also impacts our chakras in a momentous way. Depending on our food choices, we can either bring positive healing to our chakras and flourish in life, or diminish them and experience unbalance. Even without thinking about chakras, foods, in general, can also help us to live the most beautiful and most enriching lives we can possibly live.

Eat like your life depends on it!

—MARK SISSON

🕊️🕊️🕊️
A Vessel of Love & Peace

When consuming food, it should be in the best quality, as food is energy and nutrition. Getting your nutrition right is one of the best things you can do for yourself. Our brains use twenty to thirty percent of the calories we consume, and when our brains work well, our bodies work well. Eating healthy is a form of self-love. If your food is not the best, then you cannot be your best. And I've made the decision that I want to be the best person I know how to be—not just to others, but to myself. Your relationship with yourself, and the love you have for yourself influences all the other relationships that will come in and go out of your life. The great Kundalini teacher Yogi Bhajan said, "If you can't see God in all, you can't see God at all." This includes within yourself!

Several weeks into my yoga practice, I overheard Silvia talking about her local health angel, and I immediately knew that this was no coincidence. I had prayed to be led to the right holistic doctor, and when she called him an angel, I knew he was my answer. When I went onto his website and felt it speak to me, I called the office that afternoon and scheduled an appointment for myself and my husband. A few weeks later, we headed out for a consultation, wherein the doctor would analyze our blood work, and discuss his program in further detail. I prayed on the way there that my husband and I would have complete peace and clarity.

    Our diets were already pretty good, but I knew there was still room for improvement. I knew there were still things in our diet that were not serving our highest good, because my husband and I both were too young to feel as tired as we did. After reviewing our blood work and doing a few holistic testing methods, my husband did not hesitate one bit on committing to going under their care for the next eight months. We completed a complete cellular detox from a holistic approach.

Dr. Jim has been a true blessing to my family. He graduated Cum Laude from Life Chiropractic College as a Doctor of Chiropractic. He has been practicing for over forty years. He uses an approach and protocol that allows the body to heal naturally, which patients call "miracles." His program has been immensely and unbelievably life-changing. He truly believes God works through him to heal his patients. His mission and lifework are to help people learn the truth from a holistic approach, and help give his patients back the quality of life that they deserve.

According to research, the benefits of chiropractic care may consist of:

- An improved immune system.
- An improved digestive system.
- An increase in energy.
- Lowered blood pressure.
- Better breathing.
- And an improvement of eighty percent of ailments when the structure of the body

is properly aligned to allow a free flow of vital energy.

Dr. Jim first put my husband and me on a ketosis diet to remove the yeast from our bodies. During the first two weeks, we both experienced keto flu symptoms.

On week three, I looked at my husband and asked him, "Do you feel as good as I do, and as clear-minded as me?"

"Yes, and yes!" he answered. "I feel absolutely amazing!"

Today, I am processed sugar-, yeast-, and gluten-free. The basis of my diet consists of organic, non-GMO foods, such as: meat, fish, bone broth, plenty of water, eggs, ghee, fermented foods, nuts and seeds, healthy oils, avocados, plenty of veggies, fruit in moderation, and anything from the coconut. I have full faith in the way I treat my body. I am no longer tired or anxious. My body is a vessel in which I spread love and peace. I have no recollection of ever feeling this good.

Nourishing Our Bodies

Saint Germain puts it best in his teachings from the *I AM Discourses*: "You can positively produce whatever you want in your body if you want to fix your attention upon the Perfection of it—but do not let your attention rest on the imperfections."

Similarly, Rhonda Byrne says, "It is vital that whenever you have a negative thought or feeling about the current state of your body or health, that you replace it immediately by visualizing yourself with the ideal state you want, and by being truly grateful as though you have already received it."

Foods that I have found to be most healing to the body are anything from the coconut, freshly squeezed celery juice, bone broth, wheatgrass, fresh herbs, collagen, and magnesium.

A little bit of background on coconut: throughout human history, it has been called variations of "the tree of life." This is because nearly every part of it can be consumed, or be used for something. In the language of Sanskrit, it is called *kalpavriksha*, or "tree of heaven." It is for this reason that each day, I take a dose of coconut kefir with MCT oil. I also often add coconut water to weekly smoothies, as well as cook with coconut aminos, and coconut milk. The MCT oil that I take is made of medium-chain triglycerides that help with healthy weight loss. This particular oil also helps in the suppression of hunger, improvement of brain functions, strengthening of the gut, and boosting of energy levels.

Coconut kefir is made from coconut water that has been fermented with kefir grains. This nourishes the digestive tract with thriving probiotics, boosting the strength of your immune system. Probiotics are essential for breaking down food, taking in nutrients, improving digestion, fighting sugar cravings, and protecting us from unhealthy bacteria. This, overall, promotes great health and the feeling of living it out, as well. The name "kefir" comes from the Turkish word *keif*, which means, "good feeling."

Celery is a powerful anti-inflammatory food that I enjoy having as a part of my diet. It starves unproductive bacteria, yeast, mold, fungi, and viruses present in the body. Celery juice also revives liver cells, flushes out toxins, flushes out pharmaceuticals, metals, petrochemicals, pesticides, and herbicides. Consuming celery juice is the most powerful way to alkalize the gut. Sixteen ounces is the magical number. Medical Medium has said that, "If people knew all the potent healing properties of celery juice, it would be widely hailed as a miraculous superfood."

Bone broth stock has been observed to be the main thing you can consume to treat leaky gut syndrome, overcome food intolerances and hypersensitivities, improve joint well-being, diminish cellulite, and boost the immune system. It has over nineteen easy-to-absorb, essential and non-essential amino acids; collagen/gelatin, which helps form connective tissue; and nutrients that support digestive capabilities, immunity, and brain health. Bone broth benefits every part of your body, from your muscles to your gut to your ligaments. It might as well be called "nature's multivitamin." Similar to it is wheatgrass, which is an effective healer inside and outside of the body. It contains all minerals known to man.

Next, collagen. My personal favorite collagen is the TruMarine collagen from WithinUs. Collagen is one of the most abundant proteins in the body. It contains important amino acids that are used by the body to build connective tissue structures, which in turn, supports the functioning of our cells. Starting in our early twenties, we begin to lose approximately one percent of our collagen each year. Collagen is responsible for giving the skin elasticity; hair, nails, joints, and bones their strength; and connective tissue its ability to hold everything in place. Benefits from taking collagen include: glowing skin, a more youthful appearance, joint health, tendon and bone strength, healthy cartilage, improved digestion, gut health, deeper sleep, and boosted metabolism and thyroid hormone levels.

Last, but not least is magnesium. My husband and I take the Natural Vitality Natural Calm Magnesium. This is because magnesium is one of the most important minerals in the body, and is needed for optimal energy levels. It is essential for cellular health, and is a critical part to over six hundred biochemical functions within the body. Dr. Norman Shealy, M.D., Ph.D., an American neurosurgeon has stated that "every known illness is associated with a magnesium deficiency, and it is the missing cure to many diseases."

I also do intermittent fasting quite often. Intermittent fasting is an eating pattern that cycles between periods of fasting and eating. Basically, I eat during a six-to-eight hour window, and then fast for the other sixteen-to-eighteen hours of the twenty-four hour day. This allows your digestion time to rest and rejuvenate. When you fast, several things happen within your body on a cellular and molecular level: human growth hormone levels go up and insulin levels go down; your body's cells change the expression of genes; initiate cellular repair; and boost your metabolism.

Fasting has been practiced throughout human evolution, whether for religious and spiritual reasons, or for survival. Ancient hunter-gatherers did not have a choice because food was far more scarce. Breakfast actually breaks down into break+fast. In fact, intermittent fasting is more natural than always eating three, four, or more meals per day.

Nutrition is not about being low-fat. It is also not about being low-calorie. Nor is it about being hungry and feeling deprived. It is nourishing your body with real, whole foods, so that you are consistently satisfied and energized to live life to the fullest.

Gratitude is a vaccine, an antitoxin, and an antiseptic.

—JOHN HENRY JOWETT

Primary Foods

A beautiful article I came across online best summarized my relationship with primary foods. It went a little like this:

"Think back to a time when you were passionately in love. Everything was exciting. Colors were vivid. You were floating on air, gazing into your lover's eyes. Your lover's touch and shared feelings of exhilaration were enough to sustain you. You forgot about food and were high on life. Remember a time when you were deeply involved in an exciting project. You believed in what you were doing and felt confident and stimulated. Time seemed to stop. The outside world faded away. You did not feel the need to eat. Someone had to come by and remind you.

"Imagine children playing outside with friends. At dinnertime, the mother reminds the children, 'Time to come in

and eat.' 'No, mommy, I am not hungry yet,' they responded. At the end of the day, the kids return, exhausted, and go to sleep without thinking about food at all. This is living on primary food. The same as when deeply in love, or working passionately on a project. The fun, excitement and love of daily life have the power to feed us so that food becomes secondary.

"Primary foods feed us, but they don't come on a plate. Elements such as a meaningful spiritual practice, an inspiring career, regular and enjoyable physical activity and honest and open relationships that feed your soul and your hunger for living all constitute for primary foods. The more primary foods we receive, the less we depend upon secondary foods. The opposite is also true. The more we fill ourselves with secondary foods, the less we are able to receive the primary foods of life.

"Every spiritual tradition encourages people to fast during the year so that individuals have time to reduce secondary foods, thus allowing

for a greater awareness of primary foods."

This is what fasting did for me. I realized that I don't need to eat as much as I had been programmed, or taught. I was finally living on primary foods again, where secondary foods were no longer as important. Since this change, life has been absolutely riveting, and I have gratitude for it all.

Part Five:
Living Deeply

Moving Mountains

Wisdom from ancient teachings and modern times teaches us that the beginning and the end of the day is a time to think, evaluate, and correct course. This is why it is crucial to create positive rituals at the beginning and end of each day. I keep a five-minute gratitude journal next to my bed that helps me to start and end the day on a positive note. Five minutes is the ideal time window that allows for minimal effort with a magical reward.

Our minds have more power than most people understand, and it never loses its creative force. A thought and belief combined is a powerful surcharge that can literally move mountains. Meditation is one of the most powerful tools the ancient Ayurvedic physicians prescribed for balancing the mind, the body, and the spirit. Meditation taps into your imagination without limitations and your imagination is the preview to life's coming attractions. Committing to a daily meditative practice can awaken the power of your mind. There are several different meditation practices, but a few that I practice are: mindfulness meditation, movement meditation, focusing meditation, and transcendental meditation.

Mindfulness meditation is a process of being fully present in the moment with your thoughts by combining concentration with awareness. It is a way to strengthen your connection to your our own inner voice. Mindfulness meditation can be instrumental in helping to overcome dissatisfaction, impatience, intolerance and many other habits that keep us from living fuller, happier lives. Mindfulness practices have been shown to reduce depression, stress, and anxiety.

Movement Meditation focuses on the body in motion. Walking meditation, yoga, tai chi, and martial arts are all types of movement meditation. This practice encourages you to focus less on distractions, and to concentrate and stay more in the moment. The movement of your body is the object of this meditation. Having a commitment to some form of physical discipline is very beneficial.

Focusing Meditation involves focusing on whatever it is that you are doing. In this form of meditation, you simply refocus your awareness each time you notice your mind wandering, back to the task at hand. Through this process, your ability to concentrate improves. Breathing is a form of focus meditation; it is a subconscious behavior, but to the more enlightened being, the breath is energy, which can be used to our advantage. We all have the same energy, but how we use our energy makes all the difference.

The "transcendental" part of "transcendental meditation" simply means *to transcend.* It is a form of a silent mantra, either 'I am Divine Consciousness," or 'Thank you that I am____." This is practiced for twenty minutes, twice per day, while sitting with your eyes closed, and focusing on your third eye. The goal of this type of meditation is the state of enlightenment. It does not focus on breathing, or chanting, like other forms of meditation. Instead, it encourages a restful state of mind beyond thinking. It is a simple, natural, and effortless technique for recharging your mind and body, and creating a brighter, more positive state of mind. Through this, you are allowing your mind to easily settle inward, through quieter levels of thought, until you experience the most silent and peaceful level of your own awareness—pure consciousness, or The Gap. The most elusive space for human beings to enter is the gap between our thoughts, because it is through there that we make contact with God through meditation.

Be still and know that I am God.

—PSALMS 46:10

The Gap

Wayne Dyer says, "We need the void of nothing in order to create something. Without the void, there would be noise all the time. It is the silence between the notes that makes the music." In the silence between our thoughts, we find the possibilities of creative genius and spiritual awareness. Our thoughts require pause in between them to give them life to what they represent separately. This is the gap, and it's space that allows us to build, create, imagine, and manifest all that we are capable of creating with those thoughts. It is a place of ecstasy, peace and serenity."

Dyer also said that he "thinks of the gap as God's house, since God is omnipresent, invisible force that is in all of creation. Within us is the most unfathomable power to enter the gap between our thoughts, where we can commune silently with God and bring to life the same creativity that we see in the world of nature. We are just as much a part of the miraculously creative panorama of nature as the flowers, the sunsets, the seedlings turning into palm trees, the changing of the seasons, and everything else. It is being outside of the gap, and listening only to the ego that keeps us from living at the level of being able to manifest."

The root chakra and the third eye chakra are the two essential manifestation chakras. The root chakra has an internal invisible channel that goes from the base chakra to the third-eye. Within the final weeks of manifesting this book into the world, I committed myself to Wayne Dyer's Manifesting Your Destiny meditation practice. This involved twenty minutes of meditation at sunrise to the sound of "*AH*," and focusing on my heart's deepest desires. *AH* is the sound of creation, and is the only sound that takes no effort. It is the sound that occupancies co-creation from the root chakra to the opening of the third eye chakra.

Then at sunset, I commit to twenty minutes of meditation to the sound of "*OM.*" *OM* is the Word of God, and during this evening, meditation I focus only on gratitude. The sound of *OM* is a vibration, which connects us to the Divine with increased puranic energy. Form and creation come from vibration. Both of these meditations are more about the vibrational content than the meaning. *OM* is known to be the most elemental of vibrations, it is the prime mantra of the Higher self, and it attunes us with our true nature.

David Lynch says, "That if you have a golf ball sized consciousness, then when you read a book, you will have a golf ball sized understanding; when you look out a window, you will have a golf ball sized awareness; when you wake up in the morning, you will have a golf ball sized wakefulness. As you go about your day, you will have a golf ball sized inner happiness, but if you expand your consciousness, then when you read a book, you will have more understanding; when you look out the window, you will have more awareness; when you wake up, you will have more wakefulness. As you go about your day, you will have more inner happiness. You will catch ideas at a deeper level, and creativity will really flow. It makes life more magical."

He also says, "Other forms of meditation will keep you on the surface. You will not transcend and you will not get to the fourth state of consciousness, and you will not get that bliss. Transcending is its own unique thing; it is total brain functioning. When you dive within the self, you experience true happiness; pure bliss. Physical, emotional, mental, and spiritual happiness that starts growing from within; negativity diminishes and you gain a far more understanding of all aspects of life."

❦❦❦
Our Inner Holiness

Transcendental meditation is indeed truly powerful, and my favorite type of meditation. Its power is so magnificent, that if one percent of a population in any given area were to practice this together, then that one percent would have the power to improve the quality of life of an entire population. This is called the Maharishi Effect. It is one of the most widely practiced and among the most widely researched meditation techniques.

When transcendental meditation is done properly, it is equivalent to four hours of sleep, although sleep is still crucial to our overall well-being. When we don't get enough sleep, our mediations become duller. If you are well-rested, however, you will have a clearer, deeper experience. Through lots of research, I've also found that this type of meditation is said to be three times deeper of a rest than that of your deepest sleep. This is incredible news. Some may decide to consult with a transcendental meditation expert to effectively learn this type of meditation. However, I believe just like anything else, the more that you practice a skill, the better you'll become at it.

Romans 12:12 tells us to "not be conformed to this world, but be transformed by the renewal of your mind." This applies when we reach a higher level of consciousness. Divine consciousness is the consciousness of a higher self that is pure peace, bliss, and divine power. Human consciousness feels that there is nothing more important than earthly pleasure. Divine consciousness, however, is a heavenly place that knows that there is nothing more important, or significant, than heavenly joy and bliss here on Earth. Divine consciousness makes us feel that God is right here, inside each life-breath, inside each heartbeat, inside everyone and everything around us. In human consciousness, there is not a purpose, but there is a yearning or knowing that there has to be more.

When our feelings are filled with worry, anxiety, fear, and doubt, we demonstrate that we do not trust our Inner Holiness. In a lower level of consciousness, we stumble around on our own, with feelings of pain and hurt, without understanding or knowing. When we trust in our inner Holiness, though, we live from higher levels of consciousness—Heaven on Earth.

Additionally, theta meditation is one of the more elusive, yet extraordinary brain states. It is also known as the twilight state, in which you normally only experience for a short-lived time as you're waking up, or as you're drifting off to sleep. Theta is the brain state where the magic happens. In this state, you are in a waking dream. Receptivity is heightened here, and you are able to access knowledge and information that lies beyond your conscious awareness.

Deep insight was developed to help you access those higher levels of creativity that are essential to finding the answers for which you are longing and searching. These are answers you cannot find in books, or from other people. Instead, they are the true answers that reside within your own subconscious mind. Theta rests directly on the threshold of your subconscious and it is the gateway to the Universal Mind. In it, flashes of vivid imagery dance before your mind's eye, you may feel a floating sensation as your mind expands beyond the boundaries of your body. You can access theta meditations online as well.

      Lastly, other forms of meditation that I am interested in practicing are Kundalini, guided visualization, Qi Gong, and heart rhythm meditation. I know that these are all unique, and can help to bring better awareness, as well as true enlightenment.

You should sit in meditation for twenty minutes every day; unless you are too busy, then you should sit for an hour.

—ZEN SAYING

A Vision of the Night

When we sleep, we often dream. The dreams we have influence our chakras, since our thoughts are connected to our senses and our emotions. Our dreams are either giving us peace, or creating stress during our sleep. In our dreams, we're trying to work through things that we subconsciously consider unfinished. This is why it's often said that meditation and breathing practices that focus on the heart chakra are best before sleep, and also why we should always resolve any unfinished business before sleep.

Use the last moments of your day to reinforce in your mind that your heart's desires are fulfilled. It is in sleep that you enter the world of your subconscious mind, and it is here were you will receive your instructions, as indicated in the Bible: "In a dream, in a vision of the night, when deep sleep falls upon men, while slumbering on their beds, then He opens the ears of men, and seals their instruction" (Job 33:15-16).

Here is what Wayne Dyer addresses regarding sleep in his book *Wishes Fulfilled:*

"Sleep is the natural state for your subconscious mind, which rules about ninety-six percent of your waking life. The last five minutes of your day before you enter into your sleep state are the most important five minutes of your day. In this brief portion of your day, you are going to tell your subconscious mind how you feel and what wishes God (the universal one subconscious mind) is to fulfill upon awakening from a deep slumber. The five-minute segment of time in your bed, about to enter into your subconscious and marinate for the next eight hours or so, is the most crucial segment of your entire twenty-four hour day. Impress upon your subconscious mind; therefore, the mind of God to which you are eternally joined, your conception of yourself as a Divine creator in alignment with the one mind. Your slumber will dominate your last waking concept of yourself. The last thought that you have in your mind can last up to four hours in your subconscious mind."

His spiritual soul mate and advisor Neville Goddard says similarly: "Your subconscious gives form to your desires only when you feel your wish fulfilled. How would you feel if your wish was already realized? This is the feeling which should monopolize and immobilize your attention as you relax into sleep. You must be in the consciousness of being or having that which you want to be or to have before you drift off to sleep."

And finally, his spiritual teacher, Omraam Mikhael Aivanhov says, "It is the experience of the last minutes before you go to sleep that is more important, more significant, than everything that happened during the day, and never go to sleep with negative thoughts in your mind, for they will destroy all the good you may have gained during the day."

*Part Six:
Nosara*

In Harmony

One morning, after my yoga practice, I looked at Silvia and said, "I am living Heaven on Earth,"

"Why do you keep saying that?" she asked.

"Silvia, that is how I feel!"

Later that afternoon, I called to tell her that I was being pulled to start a blog, and I wanted her opinion on the name. "Should it be 'Heaven On Earth,' or 'I Am Living Heaven On Earth'?" I asked. We both agreed that "Heaven On Earth" would be better.

In the meantime, I sent a text to another friend that I recently had met at the nail salon. We would text occasionally and I felt led to text her that I was starting a blog named "Heaven On Earth." She immediately texted back and said, "That domain is available," and advised me to go ahead and purchase it. She also said, "It is available on Instagram, and you should get that one, too." She then sent me a direct link to Google Domain, which spoke to me because of its green and blue colors, the same colors that keep reappearing as colors that guide me.

After I had arrived home that afternoon, I felt pulled like a magnet to my computer. I clicked on the Google Domain link and purchased the domain name, "I Am Living Heaven On Earth." It happened so fast, that I did not even feel as though I was the one that just made the purchase. I had energy flowing through me that was so powerful; I was on such a high.

An hour later, I called Silvia again to talk about something that had dawned on me. "Silvia, I just realized that I purchased the wrong domain name. We talked about this and we agreed on 'Heaven On Earth.' I purchased 'I Am Living Heaven On Earth,' instead."

"You are not going to believe what I'm looking at as you're telling me this."

"What?" I asked.

She continued on. "I am standing in front of a car that has a magnet on the side of it that says, 'Trust the hands of Christ.'" She then sends me a picture of it, and says, "It is meant to be: 'I Am Living Heaven On Earth.'"

"I have to leave it!" I said. "After all, 'I Am' are the two most powerful words in the Universe. I believe it is meant to be 'I Am Living Heaven On Earth.'" I did not have a clear path, or even know exactly why I purchased the domain name. Having faith and not seeing the big picture was a bit scary, but to have such peace was exciting.

A few days later, I was at my appointment with the orthodontist. While I was there, my orthodontist received a text message and said aloud, "That is strange. That is a friend of mine that I have not heard from in a while that purchases domain names and hangs onto them, and sells them for substantial large amounts of money,"

Hearing this, I thought to myself, *Did I purchase this domain name to hang on to it and sell it?* I was a bit confused for a minute, but I have not been pulled in the least bit to do anything with the domain. One day, it will all make sense, but for now, I will stay in harmony with the flow of life.

Faith is taking the first step even when you can't see the whole staircase.

—MARTIN LUTHER KING, JR.

A Trip to Remember

As I continued attending my yoga classes, I was building special bonds with these women. Special enough that Tammie, my instructor, asked me if I would be interested in going on a yoga retreat with her to Costa Rica. My first instinct was to say that there is no way my family can survive for eight days without me. I am the one that runs the household, while my husband runs the business. I briefly mentioned it to my husband, and he immediately agreed that there was no way. After that, I did not give it much more thought. I trusted that if I were meant to go, then somehow a way would be made for it to happen.

As the retreat date got closer, however, I was feeling tugged within, so I prayed and asked God to give me clarity and peace regarding the situation. Three weeks prior to the trip, Tammie and Silvia arrived at my house on a random occurrence. While they were there, Tammie spoke with my husband about the Costa Rica trip; and out of nowhere, my husband looked at me and said, "Honey, I think you should go."

My heart skipped a beat. "Really, I do feel that I am meant to go, but who will take care of everything that I take care of?"

"We will figure it out," he insisted. "And it'll be good for the kids to be without you. It will teach them to be more independent."

"Okay, I am going!" I said, and the next day, I had everything booked and scheduled. I knew I was supposed to go; therefore, I had complete peace. This was the first time I had left my family duties in fourteen years.

Three weeks later, I flew off to Nosara, Costa Rica on a yoga retreat for eight days. From the moment I arrived there, the whole experience was nothing short of heavenly and magical. There was constant moisture in the air that kept my skin soft and lush, so much so that there was no need for lotion of any kind.

I did not have to add filters to my photos because the lighting was perfect. There were animals and vibrant flowers everywhere we went. The plants in the rainforest held healing powers within their roots, stems, and leaves. The food even tasted and looked divine, having delightful aromas fill the air. Everyone that I encountered spoke of magic; I even met a friend whose name was Magic. The people there treated each other like brothers and sisters. No one seemed to be anxious or in a hurry. Once there, anyone could easily feel the elevated consciousness.

  I laughed and cried during the entire trip. I was at a loss for words because words can not describe the details. I roomed with an Earth angel named Kim, a person that talks outwardly about all of her thoughts. At night, she would rest in bed in amazement, reflecting on the experiences that we had.

  One night she asked me, "How do we even go back home and tell people about things that have happened to us here?"

"You don't. They will never understand," I told her.

The Costa Rican culture has a deep connection with the natural world. Residents know the names of the animals, the medicinal uses of the plants, and treat the land with respect. They have a love for Mother Earth and live in harmony with one another. Their sunsets are magical, their water has the highest calcium content, and they keep their focus on the family. They ingest fewer calories than Americans do by having a light dinner early in the evening. They maintain healthy social networks; receive adequate sun exposure, so that their bodies produce good Vitamin D with fewer respiratory diseases; engage in regular physical activities; and have many successful centenarians that live there.

Costa Rica is one of the five Blue Zones. Coined by Dan Buettner through his book, *The Blue Zones Solution*, areas like these are where the healthiest people in the world live. Research links their increased longevity to a Mediterranean diet, which is heavy in vegetables, healthy fats, and contains smaller amounts of dairy and meat. There are nine commonalities of people that live in the Blue Zones: they move naturally, they have a purpose, they belong, they put family first, they have daily downtime, they eat until they are eighty percent full, they have moai groups, they drink wine with friends in moderation, and they eat mostly vegetables.

Centenarians have a strong sense of purpose, feel wanted and needed, and aim to contribute to the greater good. The Happy Planet Index ranked Costa Rica as "the happiest place on Earth." In this country, the moments consume you and being present is easy. That is when you feel the magic that has been within you all along.

To First Heal Ourselves

Our coolest experience happened while we were on our bike outing. Out of nowhere, Tammie's bike chain broke. The other girls that were with us wondered aloud, "What are we going to do?"

"Don't worry, an angel will rescue us," I assured.

They thought I was silly. However, about that time, a beautiful blonde-haired, blue-eyed woman on a four-wheeler rode up right next to us. "Do you ladies need help?"

"Yes, of course! You are our angel here to help us," I said.

She knew exactly what to do, and then proceeded to ask, "Where are we headed?"

"We would love to find a local jewelry shop," we said as a group.

"Well, follow me," she said. "You're in luck. I happen to own one of the local jewelry shops." Her shop was closed that day, but she let us in anyway, and we spent over two hours with her. The whole experience was pure magical; a divine appointment.

Emily Hamilton Laux is her name, and she is the owner of Adorning Aphrodite, a shop that sells one-of-a-kind jewelry to inspire the soul. From her shop, I purchased a Lemurian crystal, a blue Angelite stone, a Fulgurite, a garnet stone, a Tibetan quartz, and a white topaz necklace. I was unaware of their meanings, until I dug deeper, especially after coming across an Instagram post from @iamsahararose. The post was a picture of the lost land of Lemuria on an Oracle Card from Rebecca Campbell's *Work Your Light* Oracle Card deck. On it were the words: "Creating Heaven on Earth. It's happening."

This literally took my breath away, and I think my heart skipped a beat. A few months prior, a friend mailed me the exact same deck of cards. I immediately went into my guidebook, and this is what I found:

Lemuria or Mu is one of the Earth's lost lands, where heaven really was a place on Earth. A time before we were kicked out of the Garden of Eden. In Lemuria, life worked in harmony, all beings were seen as equal and we were deeply reverent to Mother Earth. We knew that a mosquito was no worse than us and the sun no better.

Perhaps you, too, believe that heaven really can be a place on Earth. Perhaps you are part of the transition team who at a soul level are devoted to creating this kind of harmony on the planet now. Thank you for wanting to do this work. It's easy to get overwhelmed by the state of affairs on the planet right now, but you are being encouraged to keep holding the clear vision of the future; it is closer than you think.

You may be guided to hold the frequency of Lemuria in your own community, family, workplace, or within yourself. Know that it is possible, and while at times it may feel like you are alone, you truly are not. There are hundreds of thousands who hold the codes of this ancient lost land and even Lemurian crystals that hold the codes of remembering that are beginning to rise all over the planet.

Keep doing what you are doing and remember: The only way to heal the world around us is to first heal ourselves. I hold the codes of Lemuria and believe that heaven really can be a place on Earth.

— REBECCA CAMPBELL

I was in amazement—A Lemurian Quartz crystal symbolizes a stairway to heaven!

Through research, I learned the meaning behind the others I had purchased, as well. The meaning of the blue Angelite stone name comes from its strong vibration to make contact with the angelic realm. The lovely blue stone has a peaceful energy that is a calming and soothing vibration, and is known for one of the strongest stones for strengthening spirituality and spiritual awareness.

Fulgurite is formed when lightning strikes onto sandy soil or sand. Fulgurite comes from the Latin word *fulgur* which means lightning. Fulgurite is said to be a powerful manifesting tool due to its high and potent vibration. A common use for Fulgurite is for manifesting through the power of prayer, and then blowing your prayer out through the center of the hollow stone. Ask, Believe, and Receive!

The Tibetan Quartz is said to carry the vibration of OM, which harmonizes with the third eye. When the third eye chakra is opened, you view the world without judgment and you perceive things beyond the scope of your senses. Because of this quality, the Tibetan quartz connects you to your dreams.

The Garnet stone is a deeply spiritual stone of higher thinking and self-empowerment. It is also a stone of strength and safety, as well as of prosperity and abundance, encouraging gratitude and service to others. It is also known as the stone of health.

The white topaz necklace that I purchased that day is the one I wear around my neck every day. White topaz is a stone of the highest spiritual vibration. It brings your manifestations into alignment with the highest good, and it is a stone of success and a bright white light.

I think it is pretty neat to now know the energy meanings of the stones that I picked that day. The symbolic meanings are all immensely beautiful. These stones had set in my sacred box for several months, and I was unsure of why I had even purchased them until now, as I am writing this book. I now understand; they are each perfect in their own way.

After leaving Emily's shop, we found a local restaurant to have a sit-down lunch. During our meal, I searched for Emily on Instagram, and the result nearly caused me to fall out of my chair. Her jewelry page is called *Adorning Aphrodite*. Adorning means to make more beautiful or attractive, and Aphrodite is an ancient Greek goddess associated with love, beauty, pleasure, and procreation. The key words on her "adorningaphrodite" Instagram page are: "Simple Magic." Then, I went onto her Nosara, Costa Rica Instagram page @nofilternosara, and the keywords on this page are: "What can I say? It is Heaven on Earth!" I knew instantly why I was pulled to come to Costa Rica, and why I was led to her. I had changed my Instagram handle name to @iamlivingheavenonearth five days prior.

I am committed to handcrafting jewelry that resonates with the power of the natural world. Each piece can bring its owner into a deeper relationship with the magic of the Universe and has the potential to empire them to manifest their dreams.

—ASHLEY LAUX

🕊🕊🕊
Divine Appointment

Midway through my stay in Costa Rica, I received a phone call from my husband, and heard a difference in his voice. "Honey, I have to tell you what happened to me today: I had my first divine appointment!"

My knees gave out from underneath me and I fell to the ground in tears. I could tell by the sound of his voice that something magical had happened, and I knew it was what I had prayed for. He proceeded to tell me that he was led to a man through one of his clients, and this man felt a strong pull and a connection to my husband that he could not explain or understand. Without planning to, he and the man spent four hours together that day.

They discovered that their lives were very similar, and that their appointment was far greater than a flooring appointment. This man shared personal and confidential stories with my husband. He told my husband that there is a big difference in building wealth versus creating it; and that as a philanthropist, he wanted to help my husband, although he was unsure of why.

He also felt led to give my husband Bernhard Langer's putter from the 1993 Masters. Langer is a two-time Masters champion and was one of the world's leading golfers throughout the 1980s and 1990s. He was ranked number one player and established himself as one of the most successful players on the PGA Tour Championships.

This man not only has helped my husband from a financial standpoint, but from a spiritual one. My husband is humbled and grateful that their lives have intertwined. With this, I can say that there is POWER in a praying wife. One day, it will all make sense.

Part Seven: I AM

God Within Us

The day after I returned from Costa Rica, my spirit said, *Melissa, go back to Wayne Dyer's podcast.* I was drawn to one including both Wayne Dyer and Oprah Winfrey, and holy cow! It was a podcast about the power of the words "I Am." I was getting confirmation after confirmation that "I am living Heaven On Earth." "I Am" had become like my second language. I had started practicing daily "I Am" affirmations about six months prior, and every single affirmation was happening to me now.

When we use the words "I Am," it is not just a positive affirmation. In the fundamental teachings of the, *I AM Discourses* and *The Moses Code,* becoming your highest self teaches that the name of God, which is you and me, is "I AM". The "Great I AM Presence" is God dwelling in you, and the use of the I AM Presence with the understanding of what it means is entering into Christ Consciousness.

In *The I AM Discourses*, Saint Germain says, "If man will turn the 'Mighty I AM' within, knowing that God is all Perfection, and that all outer appearance is but man's creation through the misuse of the God Power, he will see at once that if he sincerely contemplates and accepts the Perfection of God, he will cause to come into manifestation in his Life and experience this same Mighty Perfection."

The Moses Code was first used to free the Israelites who were enslaved in Egypt. I AM is the name of God that he revealed to Moses when he spoke out of the burning bush. This is the moment that God established the link between Heaven and Earth that had not existed before. Moses said, "Indeed when I come to the children of Israel and I say to them, 'The God of your fathers has sent me to you,' and they say to me, 'What is His name?' what shall I say to them?" (Exodus 3:13). And God said to Moses, "I AM THAT I AM. This is what you shall say to the children of Israel: I AM has sent me to you. This is my name forever, and this is My memorial to all generations" (Exodus 3:14-15).

So when we affirm "I Am," we are really saying "God in me is…" or "God in me is the action of…" Whatever follows whether it be speech, prayer, mantra, or decree is self-realized because it is the power of God within us. The words I Am either align you with the Divine, possessing you the power to co-create with the Divine, or distance yourself from the Divine according to how you are using the words. The I Am presence can be used to free you from the bondage of your ego. The ego seeks to enslave, while your soul wishes to set you free.

Moses knew that the name God gave him was very powerful. Moses told God that even Abraham and Isaac cannot do what He was asking him to do. God replied, "Yes, but to Abraham and Isaac I did give my name" (Exodus 6:3). God is telling Moses that he is giving him something that no one has ever had before. If you can learn to harness the energy of the I AM that I AM, you will understand the real truth and real secret of manifestation. God is saying that we should claim that which we are. This is claiming your oneness with the Divine.

🕊🕊🕊
The Resurrection & The Life

The following are miracles that took place once Moses shared this name with the Israelites, as well as once he was persuading the Pharaoh to stop the enslavement of the Israelites:

- His walking stick became a serpent.
- The Nile River became a river of blood.
- Plagues of frogs, lice, flies, locusts, and others were sent throughout Egypt.
- Every Egyptian firstborn was slain.
- The Red Sea was parted and re-flooded, destroying the pursuing Egyptian army.
- The Israelites were freed from Egypt, and were led into the promised land, where all their dreams come true.

Exodus 3:8 says, "I am come down to deliver them [Israelites] out of the hand of the Egyptians, and to bring them out of that land unto a good land…flowing with milk and honey." This is the place where dreams become reality, the land of overflowing and abundance.

"It is the Spirit who gives life; the flesh profits nothing. The words that I speak to you are spirit, and they are life" (John 6:63). Jesus knew the power of the words "I AM that I AM." He knew the words "I Am" is the spirit of God working through you. Jesus even says, "Most assuredly, I say to you, he who believes in Me, the works that I do he will do also; and greater works than these he will do" (John 14:12).

Feel deep in thought, and in feeling, this statement of Jesus: "I Am the resurrection and the life" (John 11:25). According to *The I AM Discourses* of Saint Germain: "This one statement immediately turns all the energy of your Being to the center of your brain, which is the source of your

Being. You will find your mind flooded with the marvelous ideas—with the abundant, sustaining Power and ability coming into expression and use for the blessing of all mankind." This is the statement that Jesus used most in his most difficult trials.

When Jesus said, "'I AM' the Resurrection and the Life," he said, "I AM." He did not refer to the outer expression. He referred to God within, because He repeatedly said: "I myself can do nothing. It is the Father within—the 'I AM'—that doeth the works."

Jesus said, "I AM the Way, the Truth, and the Life," giving recognition to the One and Only Power—God in Action within him. He also said, "'I AM' the 'Light' that lighteth every man that cometh into the world," prefacing every statement of vital importance with the words, "I Am."

Here are some of the most powerful messages from the teachings of Jesus, in which he invokes the name of God as the prefix:

- " I AM the door. If anyone enters by Me, he will be saved" (John 10:9).
- "I AM the good shepherd" (John 10:11).
- "I AM the bread of life. He who comes to Me shall never hunger, and he who believes in me shall never thirst" (John 6:35).
- "I AM the light of the world. He who follows Me shall not walk in darkness, but have the light of life" (John 8:12).
- "I AM the way, the truth, and the life. No one comes to the Father except through Me" (John 14:6).
- "I AM the vine, you are the branches. He who abides in Me, and I in him, bears much fruit; without Me, you can do nothing" (John 15:5).
- "I AM the Alpha and the Omega, the Beginning and the End" (Rev 1:8).

For every time you say I AM not, I cannot, I have not, you are whether knowingly or unknowingly throttling that Great presence within you.

—SAINT GERMAIN

The Third Word

Jesus used the Moses Code all throughout his life here on Earth. By claiming the words "I Am," Jesus tells us that he is one with God. "But whoever is united with the Lord is one with him in spirit" (1 Corinthians 6:17). James Twyman author of *The Moses Code* states, "When Jesus came along and basically said, 'I AM God,' they responded in the harshest manner. And yet, this is the essence of the Moses Code—the realization that we are all one with God, and once realized, to act with the power and passion of God in the world. When Jesus did this, miracles followed him everywhere he went."

When God said to Moses, "I AM that I AM," he introduced himself with just two words: "I Am." Typically, that phrase needs a third word to complete the sentence. But because God is in everything, everyone, and everywhere, his name does not need a third word.

We fill in the third word all the time with automatic and subconscious nouns and adjectives, but we seldom stop to question what is following our "I Am." Dig deep into who God has called you to be. Ask the tough questions, and allow God to speak to you. Give God the final say on your third word. Only there will you find your true self.

Jesus was the full representation of the I Am Presence outlined in *The Moses Code*. *The Moses Code* has been named the most powerful manifesting tool in the history of the world. When you are using your I Am Presence in service, you are not only changing your life, but changing the world. How can you use your I Am Presence to become part of this amazing evolution? Here, at this point, I want to encourage you to read James Twyman's book *The Moses Code* for a more in-depth power of the words that God repeatedly spoke to Moses in response to His name.

The Torah is presumed to have been written some 1,300 years before the birth of Christ. These ancient spiritual teachings contain the message 'I AM that I AM," that has been encoded into our souls. The holy place where God first manifests and tells Moses to remove his shoes is where Moses discovers who he truly is by his first words to God: "Here I Am." Shortly thereafter:

- God speaks to Moses and announces his name for all future generations to know—I AM that I AM.
- Jesus, over a millennia later, acknowledges God as I Am.
- Jesus reminds us that he, too, is God with his many "I AM the Way" pronouncements.
- Jesus tells us that we are all equal with God.
- Jesus assures us that he speaks as spirit and that the flesh counts for nothing.
- Jesus tells us that we, too, can do all that he does, and greater works than him.

This is the ancient code that has existed in the world for more than 3,500 years that activated so many miraculous occurrences throughout history. It contains the magical formula used by some of the greatest leaders of all time, but has been lost for thousands of years. Many of us are already familiar with the miracles that were realized through its first applications. Why it has been hidden and unused for so long is one of the great mysteries of all ages.

The Secret to Creating Miracles

We are all in a time in which the Moses Code is being shared with everyone. You can harness its power to create miracles in your own life. "Now to Him who is able to do exceedingly abundantly above all that we ask or think, according to the power that works in us" (Ephesians 3:20). This is one of the greatest gifts God has ever given to humanity; the secret to creating miracles has been revealed.

The most vital aspect of the Moses Code is to *feel* the feeling as if what you desire is already yours. If you *feel* that you are lacking or don't have something, then it is lacking or not having that you will continue to receive. When you are aligned with the "I AM that I AM," you become one with it, and you gain the same powers as God or the Tao. As James F. Twyman says, "The Moses Code doesn't work when you ask for what you want, but rather, when you feel and know that you already have the things you are seeking."

In a similar way, I love how Rhonda Byrne puts it: "When you say 'I Am,' the words that follow are summoning creation with a mighty force, because you are declaring it to be fact. You are stating it with certainty. And so immediately after you say, 'I Am tired,' or 'I Am broke,' or 'I Am sick,' or 'I Am overweight,' or 'I Am old,' the Genie says, 'Your wish is my command.'" We are all our own genies like the Genie in the film *Aladdin*. You can find the "I Am Mantra" by Benevolent Blizz on Google or YouTube.

Proverbs 18:21 tells us that, "Death and life are in the power of the tongue, and those who love it will eat its fruits." Speaking life over myself and practicing gratitude has been the most amazing transformation! The two words "I Am" are God's name. How are the words I Am being used in your daily life? Here is how they are used in mine:

#iamlivingheavenonearth
#iamintheharmonyflowoflife #iamhealed
#iamoneness #iamanointed
#iamanarkbuilder #iammadetofly
#iamwise #iamintuitive #iamphotogenic
#iamthevioletflame #iamalightworker
#iamintellectual #iamlikeable
#iaminteresting #iaminterested
#iamcompassionate #iamunlimited
#iamambitious #iamdivineconsciousness
#iamconfident #iamallknowing
#iampresent #iampure #iamabundant
#iamaphilanthropist #iamanalchemist
#iameternalyouth #iamanamazingwife
#iamawonderfulmother #iamthebestsister
#iamthebestdaughter
#iamanamazingaunt
#iamanamazingfriend #iamontime
#iamintentional #iamadimensionalbeing
#iammagnificent #iamasuperattractor
#iamdivinelyguided #iamawanderlust
#iamcreative #iamlimitless
#iamdivinelove #iampeace
#iamnologeraslavetofear #iamgrateful
#iamhappy #iamjoyful #iamplayful
#iamadventurous #iameasygoing
#iambeautiful #iamconfident
#iamhealthy #iamholistic #iamenergetic

#iamfocused #iamdecisive
#iamconnected ##iamfaithful
#iamorganized #iamcalm #iamgenuine
#iamthoughtful #iamrooted
#iamquickwitted #iamunique
#iamblissful #iamaffectionate
#iamfortunate #iamsafe #iamworthy
#iamstrong #iampowerful #iammagical
#iamkind #iamrespectful #iamrespected
#iamhonest #iamintelligent
#iamcourageous #iamenlightened
#iamresourceful #iamtrusting
#iampositive #iamacommunicator
#iameffortless #iamblessed #iamayogi
#iamasinger #iamadancer #iamaskier
#iamflexible #iamglowingfromwithin
#iamhonored #iamhumble
#iamacocreator #iamonewithgod
#iamanambassador #iamawriter
#iamasuperattractor
#iamanumberonebestsellingauthor

Repetition is important for the subconscious mind. It reinforces our healthy desires. Every time you repeat an affirmation, the conscious mind plants the seed and the subconscious mind waters it. As Uell Stanley Andersen says,

"Everything which you can conceive and accept is yours! Entertain no doubt. Refuse to accept worry or hurry or fear. That which knows and does everything is inside you and harkens to the slightest whisper."

It is the repetition of affirmations that leads to belief. And once that belief becomes a deep conviction, things begin to happen.

—MUHAMMAD ALI

❧ ❧ ❧
To Live in the Feeling

Saying, *I am living Heaven on Earth* does very little if deep down beneath my conscious mind I believe that this is impossible. You must ask with a deep *feeling* of gratitude for what your heart desires, and believe and *feel* what you most desire as an already a present fact. You then live passionately from that blissful state. Your *feelings* are the power to your thoughts and words. *Feeling* that you have actually become which you seek, because it is within your *feelings* that the magic happens. When you *feel* good, you are radiating love which changes the vital chemical production in every cell in your body. "Call those things which are not as though they were" (Romans 4:17). God always gives us what we ask for, so stop saying and thinking about what you don't want, and expect what you do.

In her book *The Power,* Rhonda Byrne invites us all to try this way of thinking: "Imagine that you have all your desires right now. How would you live your life differently? Think about all the things you would do. How would you feel? You would feel different and because you would feel different, you would walk differently. You would talk differently. You would hold your body in a different way, and you would move differently, You would react differently to everything. Your reaction to bills would be different. Your reaction to people, circumstances, events, and everything in life would be different. Because you would feel different! You would be relaxed. You would have peace of mind. You would feel happy. You would be easy going about everything. You would enjoy your day, without giving any thought to tomorrow. That's the feeling you want to capture."

The importance of feeling is what Neville Goddard also stresses in all of his works. He says: "To live in the feeling of being the one you want to be that you shall be." In addition: "Ideas are impressed on the subconscious through the medium of feeling. No idea can be impressed on the subconscious mind until it is felt, but once felt—be it good, bad or indifferent—it must be expressed. Feeling is the one and only medium through which ideas are conveyed to the subconscious."

Wayne Dyer says, "This is a key component to mastering the art of manifestation and if you seek on the outside that which you are unwilling or unable to feel on the inside, you are seeking in vain."

Loving Ourselves

Anita Moorjani wrote the book *Dying to Be Me*, in which she shares the story of her near-death experience, and what she learned from it. She states that her most striking insight from the experience is that this life—the life we are living now on Earth—could become a heaven for us if we simply understood how it worked and what we needed to do to create that heaven as our reality. She says, "Heaven is a state and not a place." What did Jesus tell his disciples? "Heaven is right here in the midst of you" (Luke 17:21).

Eckhart Tolle says the same thing in his book, *A New Earth*: "We need to understand that heaven is not a location, but refers to the inner realm of consciousness. This is also its meaning in the teachings of Jesus. Earth, on the other hand, is the outer manifestation in form, which is always a reflection of the inner. A 'new heaven' is the emergence of a transformed state of human consciousness, and 'a new earth' is its reflection in the physical realm."

Returning to Anita Moorjani, the main message she learned from her near-death experience was to love herself unconditionally, and to be as much herself as she can be. To shine her light as brightly as she can, for that is all she needs to do or be. Nothing more. She says, "When you love yourself and know your true worth, there is nothing you cannot do or heal. She learned this when she defined all medical knowledge and healed end-stage cancer. The cancer healed when she became aware of her own self-worth.

She continues on, saying, "Remember your only work is to love yourself, value yourself, and embody this truth of self-worth and self-love so that you can be love in action. That is true service, to yourself and to those who surround you. Realizing how loved and valued you are is what healed her cancer. This same knowledge is what will help you to create a life of heaven here on

Earth. You are serving no one when you get lost in the problems of the world. So the only question you need to ask yourself when you are feeling defeated or lost is, Where am I not loving myself? How can I value myself more? Loving ourselves is absolutely necessary before we can truly love anyone. Loving ourselves is not being egotistical: it is absolutely vital to our optimal health and happiness." Matthew 19:26 tells us that with God, all things are possible; and as Wayne Dyer says, "Living from this perspective, miraculous occurrences become the norm."

I knew that was really the only purpose of life: to be our self, live our truth, and be the love that we are.

—ANITA MOORJANI

The Kingdom of God Within You

I read another book called *Zero Limits* that describes the same concept. *Zero Limits* is about returning to the zero state where nothing exists, but anything is possible, and creating wonder each moment that will be unique to you, and will create magic in your life. Joe Vitale, the author, was once a homeless man. He is now a millionaire author of numerous best-selling books, an internet celebrity, and an in-demand online marketing guru. His success came from the discovery of the ancient Hawaiian Ho'oponopono system, and sharing it with the world, so others could experience the fulfillment and happiness he feels every day.

Vitale says, "Intention is a toy of the mind; inspiration is a directive from the Divine. At some point, you will surrender and start listening, rather than begging and waiting. Intention is trying to control life-based on the limited view of the ego; inspiration is receiving a message from the Divine and then acting on it. Intention works and brings results; inspiration works and brings miracles."

Which do you prefer? We've all heard the saying, "Expect a miracle." And as Henry Miller has put it, "Don't look for miracles. You yourself are the miracle."

Ho'oponopono is a Hawaiian practice of reconciliation and forgiveness that can help restore harmony within, and with others. The process cleans the unconscious, which is where blocks reside that keep us from obtaining our desires from health, wealth, and happiness. The Hawaiian word translates into English as *correction*. Understanding that harboring resentment against others hurts the person who refuses to forgive. It is a self-help methodology that removes the mental obstacles that block your path, freeing your mind to find new and unexpected ways to get what you want out of life.

Ho'oponopono is a mantra in which one repeats the words: "*I love you, I am sorry, please forgive me, and thank you.*" It is a prayer for healing, a form of mental and spiritual cleaning that can bring about stillness and calmness to the mind. The Ho'oponopono prayer is used to heal yourself, which in return heals others. The Hawaiian tradition teaches that all life is connected. Ho'oponopono is not only a way of healing ourselves, but a way of healing others and our world. This concept teaches us to take complete responsibility for our own life and happiness. The physical universe is an actualization of your thoughts. If you want to improve your life, you must heal your life. If you want to cure anyone, you do it by healing yourself.

The book *Zero Limits* is about a Hawaiian therapist that cured an entire ward of criminally insane patients without ever meeting any of them or spending a moment in the same room. He reviewed each of the patients' files, and worked on himself during the process. As the Hawaiian therapist reviewed the patients' files, he would repeat *"I am sorry, and I love you,"* over and over again.

As he worked on himself the patients began to heal. Half of them were in shackles at the ankles or wrists because they were dangerous. There were no family visits and no one could leave the building. After a few months, patients that had to be shackled were allowed to walk freely, others who had to be heavily medicated were getting their meditations reduced, and those that had no chance of ever being released were being freed. The staff began to enjoy coming to work, absenteeism and turnover disappeared.

Today, that ward is closed. The therapist was simply cleaning the part in him that he shared with them and by him healing himself he radiated that healing energy into every patient in the psych ward. He said, "You have two ways to live your life, from memory or inspiration. Memories are old programs replaying. Inspiration is the divine giving you messages." There are four simple steps to this method. Repentance, Forgiveness, Gratitude, and Love. These forces combined have amazing power. The magic of gratitude and the power of love are the two most powerful sources in the Universe. The power is in the feeling and in the willingness of the Universe to forgive and love.

You have this same power within yourself. I recommend you make this a part of your morning ritual. I have a daily reminder that reminds me to say *"I am sorry, please forgive me, thank you, and I love you."* I have used this power as part of my healing process. I have worked on myself and I now radiate that healing energy to those around me and in the world. My level of love for myself and the world is on a new level of understanding that words are unable to describe. I live in a near-constant state of awe and gratitude.

Many people believe you can only experience perfect joy in Heaven, and that Heaven is a place you go only after you die. But Jesus said, "The kingdom of God is within you" (Luke 17:21). He also said, "Let this mind in you which was also in Christ Jesus, who, being in the form of God, did not consider it robbery to be equal with God" (Philippians 2:5-6). The greatest minds in history understood that the power of God is within. Which means that the kingdom of Heaven is in each and every one of us.

The Meek & Egoless

Gregg Braden's book *The God Code* puts forth the premise that God's name is encoded into every human being. According to Braden's research, the basic elements of DNA—hydrogen, nitrogen, oxygen, and carbon—translate into specific letters of the Hebrew alphabet (YHVG), which also translates into one of the original names of God. Braden believes that when we realize the signature of God is carried within the cells of every person on Earth, we will be able to overcome evil with good and achieve the greatest desire of every human—*peace!*

The energy of peace, love, and joy has the power to shift the world. If your highest goal is to be happy and to be loved, then make others feel happy and loved. The more happiness and love you spread, the more you will experience or receive. The world you live in will become better or worse depending on if you become better or worse. If you see the world as hard, a struggle, suffering or a threatening place, then that will be the world that you see; but, if you see the world as easy, a loving place or Heaven on Earth, then that will be the world that you see. If you see through the eyes of the soul, then the world and everything in it will appear in a different light, experiencing oneness rather than separation.

In the Sermon on the Mount, Jesus says, "Blessed are the meek, for they shall inherit the earth" (Matthew 5:5). In modern versions of the Bible, "meek" is translated as humble and/or grateful. The meek are the egoless that live in a surrendered state and feel oneness with all of creation and Source.

The Tao is a book of wisdom that has been translated more than any volume in the world, with the exception of the Bible. The 23rd verse states, "Those who follow the Tao become one with the Tao, those who follow goodness become one with goodness. Those who stray from the Tao and goodness become one with failure. If you conform with the

Tao its power flows through you, your actions become those of nature, your ways those of heaven."

Your energy either pollutes the planet or heals it, so radiate your angel mist. Allow yourself to be the happiest person that you know, to live a story that lets others live better. Your enlightenment, and everyone's enlightenment, depends on it. When you are in a state of joy, you leave a positive imprint on the world. People will want to be around you because they feel elevated in your presence. Possibly not even knowing why. In this state, you become more vibrant, energetic, attractive, smarter, and sharper. This is all in line with our true nature: to be kind and loving towards all of creation.

A person that achieves this level of God-realization is able to impact everyone they encounter simply by their presence. It has been said, "That the presence of Jesus, St. Francis, and Mother Teresa could elevate the consciousness of everyone they encounter." This is the kind of consciousness, and love that I aspire to be! Heaven on Earth: Perfecting the *art of being;* this is a state of consciousness rather than a place you enter when you die. Being of such purity that even wild animals are tamed by your steadfastness, pure Christ consciousness."

When you are steadfast in your abstention of thoughts of harm directed toward yourself and others, all living creatures will cease to feel fear in your presence.

—PATANJALI

*Part Eight:
Living Heaven
on Earth*

Meant to Shine

John Heider, the author of the Tao of Leadership, describes this as a ripple effect: "Your behavior influences others through a ripple effect. If your life works, you influence your family. If your family works, your family influences the community. If your community works, your community influences the nation. If your nation works, your nation influences the world. If your world works, the ripple effect spreads throughout the cosmos."

Life is about love, purpose, passion, and meaning. These are at the core of our beings. Every soul desires love, meaning, purpose, and belonging to a powerful connection and to what really matters. The longing of the soul becomes more and more persistent until you can no longer deny its call and there is nothing in the *outside* world that can satisfy the longing that you feel. "What good will it be for a man if he gains the whole world, yet forfeits his soul?" (Matthew 16:26).

    We all have a dharma, or different path, but with the same core purpose. Our core purpose is to be of service, whether that is to heal, teach, inspire, write, make music, or engage in things just as beautiful. When we are of service, our endorphins and enzymes amplify our immune system, making us stronger, slowing down our aging process, and breaking down the separation between one and another. When we activate our potential and express our purpose, we remain in a higher state of bliss. Suffering comes when you only focus on yourself without being of service to others, the world, or when you disconnect yourself from the larger cause at hand.

    In Viktor Frankl's book, *Man's Search For Meaning,* he states that our primary drive in life is not pleasure, but the discovery and pursuit of what we personally find meaningful. The meaning comes when you do something that points, or is directed to something, or someone other than yourself. This is through giving yourself to a cause, serving another person, and loving.

Live your purpose, follow your dreams, and follow your heart. Your purpose is to create with your unique gifts and skills your unique version of what Heaven on Earth looks like to you; becoming the person that you aspire to be. Your full faith and belief in your dreams|visions will pave the way. I love what John Ortberg says in his book, *If You Want To Walk On Water, You've Got To Get Out Of The Boat*: "The worst failure is not to sink in the waves; the worst failure is to never get out of the boat." Similarly, Proverbs 29:18 says that "When there is no vision, people perish." Your life's purpose is unique and specific to you, like a perfect piece of a larger and perfect puzzle. Your life purpose will find you, and when it does, then you will know that you are walking the path that you came here to walk, and that you are doing what you came here to do—to create your Heaven on Earth.

From researching, here are the top eleven regrets of those who are dying:

- Firstly, never pursuing their dreams and aspirations.
- Wishing they would have trusted in God more.
- Working too much and never making time for family.
- Never making more time for their friends.
- Not saying "I love you" as often as they should have.
- Not expressing their feelings more, instead of holding them back, and becoming resentful towards people and things.
- Not becoming the bigger person, and resolving their problems.
- Wishing that they would have had children.
- Wishing that they had saved more money for retirement and had taken better care of themselves.
- Wishing that they would have had the courage to live true to

themselves, and not the lives others expected of them.
- Wishing that they would have known earlier that happiness is a choice.

We all came here with music to play. Don't let that music be buried with you. I cannot look back with regret, with a shriveled soul, with forgotten dreams, with an unopened gift, never following my calling. What I have learned to be true is that playing small does not serve me, my family, my friends, nor does it serve the world. There is nothing enlightened about shrinking so that other people will not feel insecure around you. This was something that I struggled with for so long, but I now know I am meant to shine, and I will not dim my light any longer. We are God's ambassadors!!!

We are all meant to shine. We are born to manifest the glory of God that is within us. It is not just in some of us; it is within all of us. When we let our own light shine, we unconsciously give others permission to do the same. As we liberate ourselves from our own fear, our presence liberates others. Being brave wins battles you cannot see, because your bravery strengthens others to win their own battles.

Don't live the same year 75 times and call it a life.

—ROBIN SHARMA

Bridging Heaven & Earth

My daily routine consists of waking up in a state of gratitude, and being thankful to have been given another day of life; our life is a gift, and every day is a gift. Then, I give thanks for my entire day going well, and for the best news that I am going to receive before I receive it, and I live it. By the law of attraction, I must receive back good news, and experiences going well. After that, I spend time reading a chapter out of *The Magic,* or whatever book that I am currently reading. Once I'm finished, I practice heart magic as I read over my magical to-do list and top desire, not knowing the how, but feeling deeply grateful from my heart that it is complete. Next, I spend time in a twenty-minute transcendental meditation, and in my daily prayer, I give thanks for the things I am praying for as if they are already done:

Thank you God that "I Am the Resurrection and the Life," in thought and feeling. Thank you that I am led and guided along my path today. Thank you for working through me, speaking through me, loving through me, and thinking through me. Thank you that the connection between my heart and brain are harmonized. Thank you that you occupy and have taken dominion over my superconscious, my conscious, my unconscious, and my subconscious mind!

Thank you that you have strengthened my love, my gratitude, my knowledge, my insights, my intuition, my faith, my clarity, my understanding, my courage, my abilities, and my wisdom. Thank you that you have fulfilled my hearts desires. Thank you that I only bring light into the world. Thank you that my life is an offering to my fellow brothers and sisters, and thank you for continuing to use my family and me for the greatest good for all. Thank you that you have poured miracles of healing love in my life, my loved ones, and in the lives of the multitudes all around the world.

Thank you that the kingdom of heaven has come into manifestation upon Earth. Thank you for putting an end to strife and struggle. Thank you that love has taken dominion over the world. I release the outcome to you and surrender to a plan far greater than my own understanding. Thank you, thank you, thank you!!! And so is. In Jesus' name, AMEN.

After this, I quote I Am affirmations and set my intentions for the day feeling and believing that I will find magic living from inspiration. Rhonda Byrne says, "As she goes through each day, she really feels as though she has magic power with her." This is how I feel today as well, and I encounter angels on a regular basis.

While taking a shower and getting ready, I play perfect scenarios in my mind. I imagine myself happy and having a productive day. I walk around the house in a constant state of envisioning how I want my day to play out. I visualize everything before it happens. Visualization is another powerful tool with which we have all been gifted.

      I also think about how I am going to be the best person I know how to be—not just when meeting people, but to myself. This form of conditioning can be done while performing your normal morning activities. Starting your day off in a state of gratitude, joy, and a state of certainty is a must if you want a magical life, so let there be no exception to that. It is the quickest way to be inspired and to create a lifetime of everlasting happiness. Perfect joy is God's will for us. Perfect joy is a degree of happiness neither the world nor the ego can understand, but one for which our hearts are constantly striving. This is the joy that bridges Heaven and Earth.

Our Personal Legend

When you have done your inner work and are truly inspired, everything seems to flow in a blissful state, or "In Spirit." The word *inspire* comes from "inspiration," or "In Spirit."

I believe we are here in these human bodies to learn great spiritual lessons, so that our higher self will eventually evolve into our highest self. I believe we are tested with trials and tribulations until we eventually master the lessons that we are meant to learn. Everyone on Earth has a treasure that awaits. When we master the lessons is when we receive our treasures, our dreams, our alchemy. Our highest self is not external, for the kingdom of heaven resides in each and every one of us. Think and act like God does, and you will begin to co-create, or manifest just as he does. "He who abides in love abides in God, and God in him" (1 John 4:16).

In Marianne Williamson's book, *A Woman's Worth,* she says, "A queen is wise. She has earned her serenity not by having it bestowed on her, but because she has passed her test. She has suffered, and grown more beautiful because of it. She has proved that she can hold her kingdom together. She cares deeply about something bigger than herself. She rules with authentic power." Today, I am truly humbled and beyond grateful to live in my authentic power.

See yourself as a Queen or King, carrying yourself with your authentic power. Be proud and confident in who God made you to be. You are a unique masterpiece, and He has equipped you exactly as you are supposed to be to fulfill your own personal legend.

Paulo Coelho's international bestseller *The Alchemist* is a story that teaches the essential wisdom of listening to your heart, and most importantly, to follow your dreams. He explains that to be an alchemist is to succeed at discovering your own personal legend, and that dreams are the language of God.

When God speaks in the language of the soul, it is only you who can understand.

In Coelho's words: "It is what you have always wanted to accomplish. Everyone, when they are young, knows what their personal legend is; that is when everything is clear and possible and you are not afraid to dream and yearn for everything that you would like to see happen in your life. Whoever you are or whatever it is that you do, whenever you really want something, it is because that desire originated in the soul of the Universe; it is your mission here on Earth. To realize one's personal legend, it is a person's only real obligation and when you want something, all the universe conspires in helping you to achieve it. Listen to your heart, because it knows all things, because it came from the soul of the world."

Religion of Love

I strengthen my faith daily through prayers and meditation. I meditate each day to increase my awareness of the divine power within me. Through meditation, I am able to see clearly the beauty, grace, and love that directs my life and fulfills my deepest desires. It has taken thirty-five years for me to own my beliefs fully, with certainty and understanding. The certainty that I have now is the greatest gift that I have ever received.

Today, my relationship with God transcends thought and logic, and isn't limited to any one religious tradition. I am a great believer in magic. I believe in oneness with God; I believe God's love is eternal and unconditional; I believe in angels and I believe in miracles. I believe in co-creating and I believe that there are no coincidences. I believe everything is divinely orchestrated for a far greater plan than our own understanding. In the words of Helen Schucman, I believe that if we knew who was assisting us along our journey, we would never question our own abilities.

It is my mission to share the wisdom that I have learned with the world so you can know your own certainty. Regardless, we are all spiritual beings that are here to establish a spiritual relationship with a higher power greater than our own understanding.

Recently, while I was at a nail salon, I was asked by another woman about my religious affiliation. I looked at her and said, "My religion is LOVE. I am a piece of God and God is love; as am I and as in you. I do not put a title on who I am. I am a spiritual being, just like you. Spirituality is not just based on what you believe; it is based on your state of consciousness. I do attend a non-denominational church, but I also feed my spirit daily with either a book or podcast. Religions are man-made and titles create separation in the world, but we are all one and the same."

God has no religion.

——MAHATMA GANDHI

An Instrument of Thy Peace

After being a business owner for eleven years, one thing I do know for sure is that there is nothing greater than empowering another human with your words. When we inspire, encourage, speak life over others, and encourage the good within each other, the rest will blossom. We are not here to condemn one another. People do not have to be told what they need to fix, because they already know and battle with their own faults. Give yourself the assignment to find something wonderful about every person you meet—then tell them. When you compliment another person, you compliment yourself. There is something special about everyone, and you can help them see what that is.

Words and thoughts are very powerful. When you complain, gossip, or judge another person, you are actually bringing more things to complain about, bringing harm to your own life.

Therefore, your life will be the one to suffer. By the law of attraction, whatever you think or say about another person, you bring to you. "Judge not, that you be not judged. For with what judgment you judge, you will be judged; and with the measure you use, it will be measured back to you" (Matthew 7:1-4).

In the *I AM Discourses*, I love what Saint Germans says: "The student should constantly look within his human self and see what habits or creations are there that need to be plucked out and disposed of; for only by refusing to any longer allow habits of judging, condemning and criticizing to exist, can he be free. The true activity of the student is only to perfect his own world, and he cannot do it as long as he sees imperfection in the world of another of God's children." The Bible says similarly: "Why do you look at the speck of sawdust in your brother's eye and pay no attention to the plank in your own eye? How can you say to your brother, 'Let me take the speck out of your eye,' when all the time there is a plank in your own eye?" (Matthew 7:3-4).

Monitor your speech by not uttering a negative sentiment about anything or anyone, regardless of whether you feel it is justified. Make a conscious effort to have every word that passes through your lips to be uplifting to your listener. "Let no corrupt talk come out of your mouths, but only such as is good for building up, that it may give grace to those who hear" (Ephesians 4:29). Be responsible for the energy that you bring as well as the energy that you allow from others.

I am in awe of the transformation that I have undergone. I am deeply moved by the loving and clear guidance that I receive every day, the same guidance that I have grown to completely surrender to and rely upon. As Proverbs 31:25 says, I am a woman "clothed in strength and dignity, and I laugh without fear of the future." And most wonderfully of all, I live on pure faith in a power greater than myself.

Saint Francis of Assisi prayed a prayer that has become my prayer for us all:

> *"Lord, make me an instrument of thy peace. Where there is hatred, may I bring love. Where there is wrong, may I bring the spirit of forgiveness. Where there is discord, may I bring harmony. Where there is error may I bring truth. Where there is doubt, may I bring faith. Where there is despair, may I bring hope. Where there are shadows, may I bring light. Where there is sadness, may I bring joy. Lord, grant that I comfort, rather than to be comforted. To understand, than to be understood. To love than to be loved. For it is self-forgetting that one finds. It is in forgiving that one is forgiven. It is by dying that one awakens to eternal life."*

I feel with divine love and happiness in my heart what this book will bring to millions of people. This feeling is imprinted upon my subconscious mind, and my subconscious mind creates exactly what I have come to believe and feel. I give thanks every day that this book will bring *Heaven On Earth* to the world. I have no idea how, but I surrender and trust in a power far greater than myself. I feel deep feelings of gratitude in advance for the magical outcome. *The Secret* teaches us that, "everything that has ever been invented or created throughout the history of humankind began with one thought. From one thought, a way was made, and it manifested from the invisible into the visible."

When Henry Ford was bringing his vision of the motor vehicle into our world, people around him ridiculed him, and thought he had gone mad to pursue such a "wild" vision. He, however, knew much more than the people who ridiculed him. He knew The Secret, and he knew the law of the Universe.

Ford has also been quoted saying, "Whether you think you can or think you can't, either way, you are right." I choose to think that I can. What do you choose?

❧ ❧ ❧
The Violet Flame

This all has its purpose. Saint Germain has been preparing us to enter into the Age of Aquarius for almost seventy years. This is an era of peace, freedom, and enlightenment. This is a time for all of mankind to cut free from fear, lack, sickness, and death, and instead, walk in the light as being blessed with freedom by God.

The Aquarian Age is the informational age, where nothing is a secret anymore, and all information is easily accessible. Previously, during the Piscean Age, we were dominated by hierarchy and power. The keys to life were hidden and kept a secret to only but a select few. An evolution of consciousness is occurring, however, and the Aquarian Age is opening the world up to true equality, with a knowing that we have the consciousness, knowledge, and wisdom within ourselves. We are learning to trust and love ourselves, and in turn, this creates unconditional love for one another. We are being called to value wisdom over intellect, love over fear, and connectivity over separation.

I was born on February 3rd, which makes my zodiac sign Aquarius. As the eleventh sign of the zodiac, Aquarians are the perfect representatives for the Age of Aquarius. Those born under this horoscope sign have a social conscience needed to carry us into the new millennium. Those of the Aquarius zodiac sign are humanitarians, philanthropic, and are keenly interested in making the world a better place.

Aquarians are also visionaries, and progressive souls who love to spend time thinking about how things can be better. They are also quick to engage others in this process, which is why they have so many friends and acquaintances. Making the world a better place is a collaborative effort of Aquarians.

Saint Germain, the Ascended Master for the Aquarian Age, taught us how to use the violet flame to free ourselves and all mankind. He strove to help us solve our karmic dilemmas, so that we can realize our highest potential: *I AM a being of violet fire, I AM the purity God desires.*

Dannion Brinkley, author of *Saved by the Light,* saw and experienced the violet flame in his near-death experience. He says, *"The violet flame is a light that serves all spiritual heritages, that gives respect and dignity to all things. It gives us a way to connect with each other…It is empowering!"*

The violet flame is like the sunlight passing through a prism refracting into the seven colors of the rainbow. The spiritual light manifests as seven rays. Each ray has a specific color, frequency and quality of God's consciousness. The violet flame is known as the seventh ray aspect of the Holy Spirit. When you invoke it in the name of God, it descends as a beam of spiritual energy and burst into a spiritual flame in your heart as the qualities of mercy, forgiveness, justice, freedom, and transmutation. This transmutes any cause, effect, record and memory of sin, or negative karma. When the violet flame is invoked into action, it brings about change in whatever it contacts.

By stating "I AM the violet flame," which means "God in me is the violet flame," we are transforming ourselves so that we can become more closely united with God. Saint Germain has said, "The use of the violet flame is more valuable to you and to all mankind than all the wealth, all the gold and all the jewels of this planet."

It is said the violet flame works like soap, scrubbing and dissolving anything negative that is lodged anywhere in your spiritual, or physical being. When the violet flame goes to work, it passes through the clogged spaces between the electrons and the nuclei, transforming anything negative into pure light-energy. It ejects these particles of dense substance from your body and dissolves them. This process transmutes the negative energy into positive energy and restores it to its native purity. Decrees help to remove obstacles on the spiritual path, such as fear, pride, selfishness and lack of self-esteem. When you decree, it allows God to work through you. Below is a violet flame decree from Saint Germain:

I AM the violet flame

In action in me now

I AM the violet flame

To Light alone I bow

I AM the violet flame

In mighty cosmic power

I AM the light of God

Shining every hour

I AM the violet flame

Blazing like a sun

I AM God's sacred power

Freeing every one.

Additionally, here is the I AM Presence decree:

O "I AM Eye" within my soul,

Help me to see like thee;

May I behold the perfect plan

Whose Power sets all free.

No doubt vision fills my sight,

The way is pure and clear;

I AM the viewer of the Light,

The Christ of all appears.

I AM the eye that God does use

To see the plan divine;

Right here on earth his way I choose,

His concept I make mine.

O loving Christ, thou living Light,

Help me to keep thy trust;

I AM thy concept ever right

So see like thee I must.

    I do decrees three times in a row because saying anything three times in a row is a magical formula; it is the mathematical number of all new creation in the Universe.

❧ ❧ ❧
With My Deepest Gratitude

Thank you, thank you, thank you with my deepest gratitude to the spiritual teachers, ascended masters, and angels who discovered the truths of life; and who left their written words to discover; when God aligned the stars, and caused that indefinable, life-changing moment; when I had eyes to see, and ears to hear—the moment when I became awakened! I also give my deepest appreciation to the sheer magic of gratitude, the number one practice that has abundantly changed my life, and has profoundly enriched it in the most amazing of ways!

Collaborating with forces of inspiration that I can neither see, prove, nor understand is a magical line of work that is nothing short of divine. Creativity is the relationship between a human being and the mysteries of inspiration (in Spirit). It is not just a gift to the audience; it is a gift to the creator as well. Creativity is how I choose to share my heart, soul, and gifts to the world.

This moment was made possible by years of isolation and seeking, while wondering if there truly was a God, or if I was just slipping into craziness. Months were spent in confinement. Many hours a day were devoted to typing away on my laptop, pulling together everything that had spoken to my spirit up unto this point. This moment was also made possible by my own death, so I could be born again.

I remember a time when I thought that if I lived by the teachings of the Bible, then I would not be able to live the way I wanted to, and that I would have to live a boring life. What I know now is life is a struggle, and not complete without God in it. God's plan brings success to every area of your life, causing there to be Heaven on Earth: fulfilling your hearts desires, exceeding your expectations, unfolding opportunities and dreams bigger than what you thought were even possible for yourself. My relationship with God is now the number one priority in my life. According to Wayne Dyer, "Your primary relationship needs to be with yourself. If you go there first before any other considerations, you will automatically begin to emulate the Tao, effortlessly living Heaven on Earth."

If I am being honest, there were many times I questioned myself, and wondered, *What in the world am I doing?* I felt like I was Noah building the Ark. What I know now is that I am an Ark builder! There was something inside of me telling me that if I kept strong in my faith, trusted and listened to that little nudging voice, then I would live a life beyond my wildest dreams. I knew deep down that this was bigger than me; it is my soul calling. I know I am being directed by a force far greater than myself, and I cannot erase these pictures that I hold in my imagination.

I have learned to let go of all doubt, and I have grown to learn that the pictures that I hold in my imagination are my unfolding reality all in perfect timing. In the *I AM Discourses*, Saint

Germain repeatedly reminds us that we are the masters, and have dominion in our lives. There have been times that I did not have clear guidance on my next step, but I learned that was because I was meant to keep learning; I was meant to keep educating myself, because I still needed to be a pupil. So I kept writing, I kept working, I learned to say "no," so I could stay focused on the bigger picture.

The process I have spent working on this book has been sacred, life-changing, and so fulfilling. It has expanded my imagination, and my expanded imagination has transformed my life. It has healed me, and I have evolved on a deeper level.

I was gifted anxiety and sensitivities to food so I could help others with the food body-brain relation. I was gifted others doubting me so I could be strong enough to believe in myself. I was gifted loneliness so I could seek and grow in my own faith. I was gifted independence so I would be self-reliant and make self-love a priority. I was gifted difficult relationships for an example to me of what I did not want to be. We are all gifted struggles; it is up to you on how you perceive them.

We have much to learn from every flower, every tree, every season, and every animal. They know exactly what to do without being told, and God sends them everything they need to survive. When we are aligned with Source, we, too, become magnets attracting everything we need. This means that we don't have to make things happen on our own strength. Everything flows easily and naturally to the soul when aligned. Abundance, ideal relationships, all of your hearts desires are achieved without effort. And this was my hardest, yet most enriching lesson to learn—to surrender with grace to the forces that hold me, and will continue to hold me in ways I've never dreamt possible!!!

Author's Favorites

My favorite quotes:

- "Creativity is maximized when you are living in the moment."
- "Listen, listen, listen then ask strategic questions."
- "Life is what you make of it."
- "Make the days count, don't count the days."
- "Begin each day with a grateful heart."
- "Never, never stop dreaming."
- "It always seems impossible until it is done."
- "Be somebody who makes everybody feel like a somebody."
- The best project you will ever work on is you."
- "Effort is attractive."
- "Jealousy works the opposite way you want it to."
- "What you do to the earth you do to yourself."

- "A daily hit of athletic-induced endorphins gives you the power to make better decisions, helps you be at peace, and offsets stress."
- "In any given moment we have two options, to step forward into growth or step back into safety."
- "With freedom, books, flowers, and the moon, who could not be happy?"
- "Educate yourself—When a question about a certain topic pops up, Google it. Watch movies or documentaries. When something sparks your interest, read about it. Read, read, read. Study, learn, stimulate your brain. Educate that beautiful mind of yours."
- "A wise man ought to realize that health is his most valuable possession."
- "Your day is pretty much formed by how you spend your first hour. Check your thoughts, attitude and heart."

- "Drink fresh water and as much water as you can. Fresh water flushes toxins from your body and keeps your brain sharp."
- "Make choices that bring you peace."
- "Books don't just go with you, they take you where you've never been."
- "Be the best version of you."
- "A grateful heart is a magnet for miracles."
- "A mind stretched by new experiences can never go back to its old dimensions."
- "The happiness of life depends on the quality of your thoughts."
- "Comparison is the thief of joy."
- "Since day one, she's already had everything she needs within herself. It's the world that convinced her she did not."
- "Simplicity is the ultimate sophistication."

- "Leaders aren't born. They are made."
- "The way we talk to our children becomes their inner voice."
- "Why fit in when you were born to stand out."
- "Those who leave everything in God's hands will eventually see God's hands in everything."
- "Where the spirit does not work with the hand, there is not art."
- "If you're not excited about it, it's not the right path."
- "What if I fall? Oh, but my darling, what if you fly?"
- "There are no accidental meetings between souls."
- "When you judge someone else, you cut off the creativity to your own spirit!"
- "Listen and Silent are spelled with the same letters."
- "Blessed are those who believe without seeing."

- "Your energy introduces you before you even speak."
- "Attract what you expect, reflect what you desire, become what you respect, mirror what you admire."
- "Do not be afraid of being different; be afraid of being the same."
- "To live a creative life, you must lose your fear of being wrong."
- "Elegance is when the inside is as beautiful as the outside."
- "Don't be like the rest of them, darling."
- "To live a creative life, we must lose our fear of being wrong."
- "You live but once; you might as well be amazing!"
- "In order to be irreplaceable, one must always be different."
- "When women support each other, incredible things happen."

- "Beauty begins the moment you decide to be yourself."
- "Be the person that decided to go for it!"
- "When you judge another, you do not define them, you define yourself."
- "There are no accidental meetings between souls."
- "When it is all finished, you will discover it was never random."
- "Listen & silent are spelled with the same letters."
- "Attract what you expect, reflect what you desire, become what you respect, mirror what you admire."
- "Just when the caterpillar thought her life was over, she began to fly."
- "Your energy introduces you before you even speak."
- "When women support each other, incredible things happen!"

- "I do believe something very magical can happen when you read a good book."
- "And one day she discovered that she was fierce, and strong, and full of fire, and that not even she could hold herself back because her passion burned brighter than her fears."
- "And suddenly you know… It's time to start something new and trust the magic."
- "Life becomes beautiful when you connect to your soul."
- "Be a seeker of everyday magic!"
- "Those who leave everything in God's hands will eventually see God's hands in everything!"

My top twenty-five life books that have deeply inspired me on the writing of this book:

- *The Magic* by Rhonda Byrne
- *Wishes Fulfilled* by Dr. Wayne Dyer
- *The Power* by Rhonda Byrne
- *Hero by* Rhonda Byrne
- *The Secret* by Rhonda Byrne
- *The Universe Has Your Back* by Gabrielle Bernstein
- *If You Want To Walk On Water Get Out Of The Boat* by John Ortberg
- *The Tao Te Ching (The Way)* by Lao-Tzu
- *A New Earth* by Eckhart Tolle
- *Practicing The Power Of Now* by Eckhart Tolle
- *The Moses Code* by James F. Twyman
- *The "I AM" Discourses* by Saint Germain
- *The Power of I Am* by Joel Osteen
- *Zero Limits* by Joe Vitale
- *The Untethered Soul* by Michael A. Singer
- *Big Magic* by Elizabeth Gilbert

- *Eat, Pray, Love* by Elizabeth Gilbert
- *I Can See Clearly Now* by Wayne Dyer
- *One Thousand Gifts* by Ann Voskamp
- *Conversations With God* by Neale Donald Walsch
- *The Magnolia Story* by Chip and Joanna Gaines
- *The Life Changing Magic of Tidying Up* by Marie Kondo
- *Real Magic by* Wayne Dyer
- *Super Attractor* by Gabrielle Bernstein
- *Miracles Now* by Gabrielle Bernstein

"Reading does to the mind what exercise does to the body"

—JOSEPH ADDISON

My favorite people to follow on Instagram:

- Good.tidings
- Whiteshantyathome
- Drdarylgioffre
- Jorgecruise
- Lilychoinaturalhealing
- Shaynas.kitchen
- Shaynateresetaylor
- Gabbybernstein
- thebucketlistfamily
- Iamsahararose
- Ellencharlottemarie
- Medicalmedium
- Yung_pueblo
- Benevolent_blizz
- Sincerelyjules
- Claire_grieve
- Juleshough
- kinrgy
- Bohobeautifullife

My two favorite life apps:

- Jesus Calling
- The Secret Daily Teachings

My favorite podcasts:

- Wayne Dyer
- Oprah Winfrey
- Michael Beckwith
- Gabrielle Bernstein
- Moses Code
- Abraham Hicks
- Dr. Joe Dispenza
- Joel Osteen
- Gregg Braden
- Bruce Lipton
- Ram Dass
- Billy Alsbrooks

My favorite songs:

- "Heaven Is a Place on Earth" by Belinda Carlisle
- "Firestone" by Kygo
- "Sun Is Shining" by Axwell & Ingrosso
- "Wake Me Up" by Avicii
- "Faith Hope Love Repeat" by Brandon Heath
- "A Million Dreams" by Pink
- "Different" by Micah Tyler
- "No Longer Slaves" by Bethel Music ft. Melissa and Jonathan David Helser
- "Supermarket Flowers" by Ed Sheeran
- "Heaven" by Kane Brown
- "Amazing Grace" by Celtic Woman
- "Still" by Hillary Scott
- "I Will Be What I Believe" by Blake Gillette

My energy work healing friends:

- Dr. Joan Housley with Life's Balance: "A Balanced Life Rooted in Heaven" She specializes in natural healing; helping her patients realize and live in their full potential.
- Rolene Jaffe: A Holistic Transformation Specialist, a Therapist and Journey Coach.
- Dr. Cari Cater with Tree Of Life Healing Center: A holistic approach to healing.
- David Whaley, LMT with energy-healing-atlanta.com: Reiki, Polarity, Intuitive

Author's Thank yous

It was Dr. Wayne W. Dyer, Oprah Winfrey, Eckhart Tolle, Rhonda Byrne, Anita Moorjani, John Ortberg, Bob Goff, Elizabeth Gilbert, Saint Germain, Michael A. Singer, Ann Voskamp, Elizabeth Clare Prophet, Gabrielle Bernstein, and last, but not least, my pastor Brian Bloye who have been my teachers. It is their work that has inspired me to be the woman that I am today. It was their certainty that has strengthened my own faith so I can live Heaven on Earth, and for that, I am forever grateful! These are my intentions for you and the world!!!

NAMASTE.

(The light in me recognizes the light in you, and I honor the place in you where we are all one.)

Made in the USA
Columbia, SC
04 April 2020